MANAGING YOUR E-MAIL

Thinking Outside the Inbox

———————

CHRISTINA CAVANAGH

D0059574

WILEY

JOHN WILEY & SONS, INC.

To everyone seeking their own inbox insights.

ACKNOWLEDGMENTS

Books are not written; they evolve through the help of associates, friends, and supporters. It has been my good fortune to have a legion of supporters—workplace e-mail users—to guide my hand. This legion is represented by hundreds of individuals who gave of their time to be my research subjects. The media, whose spin continued into corporate interest and guest speaking opportunities, carried their momentum.

There was a special group of people, almost an inner circle, who got me started and worked with me while this book was taking shape. The staff at the library of the Richard Ivey School of Business provided both unfailing support and a wry sense of humor; in particular, Dolly Borsato-Vassal, Patricia Hunter, and Jerry Mulcahy. Their ardor in sourcing obscure materials matched my similar sounding requests. A special note of thanks goes to Elizabeth Brixton of the Law library at The University of Western Ontario.

My heartfelt thanks and praise go to the following team who worked closely with me on the original manuscript:

- To Carol Gray, who reviewed the manuscript for context. Her insights on communicating the value and the power of the book from both individual and organizational perspectives helped to shape the finished project.

- To John Parry, an academic editor extraordinaire, who line edited the original manuscript. Little did I know he would also become a valued mentor and a guide.
- To Michael Travis, who reviewed the manuscript in detail for content. He gave very shrewd and enlightening observations and provided ongoing inspiration in developing the book.

There were a number of people who provided me with their advice, support, and encouragement during the book's growth. It would be difficult to name everyone who has contributed to my understanding of workplace e-mail.

I want to recognize those who made unique contributions, for which I earnestly offer my thanks: the late Rod Austin, Donald Barclay, Paul Beamish, Eleanor Clitheroe, Marcia Daniel, Sylvia Davis, David Estok, Peter C. Jones, Carmen Kinniburgh, Margaret McBurney, Mildred S. Myers, John Pearce, Gordon Pitts, Monique Pinnsoneault, Graham Porter, Raymond Protti, Heather Reisman, Keith Sjögren, John Stephens, Heather Whyte, Christine Wiedman, Margaret-Ann Wilkinson, and John G. Wilson. I also wish to thank Joanne Asuncion, Ruzena Andrysek, and Margaret Reffle for their administrative support.

Throughout the project, I was helped by neighbors, who took it upon themselves to look after me so I could focus my efforts on writing this book. They fed me, mowed my lawn, shoveled snow, and tended my meager garden. They also shared with me their own unique, professional perspectives on workplace e-mail. I am humbly grateful to Loraine and

Fraser Kelly, Wendy and Chris Kirwin, Pearl Pickard, and Anne and Martin Vandenbosch.

My friends and family were a lasting source of encouragement and strength. They offered valuable insight on e-mail, but they also gave me so much more—their caring, interest, and support of this project. My eternal thanks go to Trevelyn Brown, David Hague, Teri Hallahan, Sandra Hewitt, Cornelia Krikke, Linda Novik, Donna Pucciarelli, Ursula Stephens, and C. Ken Zurbrigg. I want to especially recognize the creative spirit and indomitable support of my mother Anita, who in her heart always knew there was a book in me.

The evolution of this book started with the vision of my dedicated editor—Paula Sinnott. Her constant encouragement, her artful criticisms, and her stubborn posture as the voice of the reader were a continued source of energy and stimulation for me. I am grateful, too, to Larry Alexander, Linda Witzling, Rebecca Johnson, and the rest of the superb team at John Wiley & Sons who collaborated in bringing this project to its fruition, as well as to Nancy Land and Pam Blackmon at Publications Development Company of Texas.

CONTENTS

INTRODUCTION

D o you get too much e-mail at work?

Have you ever felt that you spend more time in a day managing e-mail than managing your work? Have you ever received an incomprehensible e-mail, or wondered why you received it in the first place?

You are not alone. These questions echo throughout our office corridors. Most of us have developed a love-hate relationship with e-mail. We love it for its convenience and easy access; we hate it for its intrusive "new message" pop-up screen and almost constant demands for our attention. We love it because we can send the same message to many people with a single keystroke; we hate it because we just get too many of these messages.

This book can be your guide through this often tumultuous relationship. Applying what you read in this book will help you create a more productive union between human interaction and electronic communication. Why has this intervention become necessary? The simple answer is that e-mail use in the workplace has overtaken its original usefulness as just another way to communicate. In day-to-day workplace e-mail, it seems we've never said so much and so little at the same time.

This book takes you on a journey through the typical communication problems that occur at work and focuses on

1

the issues we face as e-mail originators and end-users every day. From this rich tapestry (which some of you may prefer to call chaos), we blend and weave practical, easy solutions that will create an immediate change in how you view and use electronic mail.

THE LEGACY OF E-MAIL

With the North American average daily volume of e-mail approaching 50 per day, our stress levels and the specter of unfinished e-mail business are ever-present. There is that odd moment of anticipation punctuated by an e-mail from a much-loved business associate or the promise of landing a new piece of business, but now these have become few and far between. Instead, most corporate e-mail inboxes are clogged daily with low value, nice-to-know information that seems to be sent just because the mechanism exists to do so.

Do you recall the first time you used electronic mail? Remember experiencing the thrill of being able to send personal letters and messages to friends and relatives around the world? E-mail seemed the next best thing to expensive travel and long-distance phone calls. We felt connected, and there was no limit to the endless threads that wove back and forth. When e-mail was more readily adapted in the workplace in the mid-1990s, we saw the same informal, chatty mode that we had used for our personal e-mails at home. As e-mail use grew in the workplace, the informal lines gave way to more professional expectations.

Several years have passed since the introduction of basic electronic mail applications and the additional capability to send attachments. Words like ubiquitous, spam, and overload have entered our lexicon. E-mail's darker side began to surface for many users.

The good news is that my own research suggests that electronic mail in the workplace may be cresting and will not significantly increase as it did during the early part of the new millennium. We are now ready to tackle e-mail from strategic viewpoints such as reducing volume and improving message content and readability. This book gives you the tools you need to take control of your e-mail. It offers perspectives and solutions for proactive management of e-mail use in the workplace. Its guiding philosophy is that "less is really more."

For me, this journey actually started in the late 1990s, when I left private industry to become an academic, joining the management communication faculty of Canada's top business school. My main focus was to teach communication strategy and skills to MBA and executive MBA candidates. The school had a strong research focus, so I set my sights on finding an area in the communications sphere that would also leverage my business background. I was fortunate to have the grassroots support of a colleague who is an accomplished researcher. We discussed the use of emoticons (those symbols put at the end of sentences to denote happy, sad, and angry moods). We found that 95 percent of all e-mail users did not use or know what an emoticon was, and that use of this symbolism, while popular in statistician and mathematical circles, was an unrecognized syntax for most.

This discovery created the first link to the current research—symbols do convey meaning, but only if there is a shared context. For instance, a person may choose to send the message "Quit being such a jerk :-)," a caustic comment with a smiling emoticon, truly meant as a humorous jibe. If the recipient has no knowledge of emoticons, then their interpretation is anything but funny. What if this same type of misunderstanding was occurring simply through use of the electronic written word?

I gathered anecdotal evidence that e-mails were indeed causing problems in the workplace. Stories abounded of abuses, inappropriate content, and inadequate control—to me, these appeared to be very relevant management issues. When this pattern kept repeating itself, I was led toward further investigation.

I asked several executives to track their e-mails for a week, indicating for each e-mail whether it fit into one of four categories—essential, relevant, low-relevance, no-relevance. My hypothesis was that 10 percent to 20 percent of e-mails would fall into the bottom two categories—low or no relevance—combined. The tabulated result was a surprising 45 percent. Shortly thereafter, a journalist from the *Toronto Star* interviewed me about this study, which in turn spawned other media and corporate interest. I now knew I had stumbled onto my research area—e-mail at work.

In the two years that followed, I responded to strong media interest across North America—print, radio, and television—as well as requests for workshops and e-mail productivity consulting. This attention reinforced the strong feelings that many people had about the problems and stresses caused by inappropriate uses of workplace e-mail. It also indicated that people were receptive to solutions. The more involved I became with these activities, the more I realized the value of this information to everyone who works with electronic mail.

Research in itself would not be enough. The research needed to be translated into a practical form. This idea became the guiding principle for this book, which:

1. Defines e-mail communication issues in the workplace
2. Uncovers the roots of the problems
3. Offers solutions that benefit both individual users and their respective organizations

This book was written for everyone who uses e-mail at work, whether they are professionals, clerical workers, managers, executives, CEOs, or entrepreneurs. E-mail users will not only identify with the problems, but will benefit from the tangible solutions offered. What makes this book unique is its practical, hands-on approach. It frames the issues in user terms, not technological terms. The book's focus is on *better communication.* E-mail is just one channel in the mix. Its misuse can wreak havoc. This book serves two closely linked audiences—the individual worker and their organization. Because of e-mail's power, a book that focused only on the individual in the workplace, excluding the workplace itself, would place the entire burden of corrective action on individuals. Organizations have a significant role to play in helping their employees be better and more productive managers of their time and energy. This mutuality between organizations and their employees demands recognition and attention—without it, there can be no real long-term solutions.

This book is designed with the busy employee in mind. It provides a much-needed refresher on all communication channels within the workplace, and then walks you through the e-mail minefield that has been created in our workplaces. We then dive into the categories and patterns of e-mail misuse, offering typical scenarios, explanations, detailed solutions, and quick tips.

One segment of the book defines the issues that organizations face in managing their e-mail networks from a strategic perspective. Ways and means are offered to minimize legal exposure, diagnose internal problems, and create meaningful policies that benefit everyone through time savings, better defined processes, and cost reductions.

This book is a reference guide to proactively managing e-mail to reduce volume, stress, and confusion. Once you read this book, you will want to recommend it to your colleagues, so they know the new e-mail rules and how to play the game to win at work. As a starting point for department discussion, specific training and workshops, and creating a movement within organizations, this book aims to make electronic mail a more effective channel for communication. Keep this guide handy and at the ready in your offices and workspaces, so you can refer to it during the course of your day-to-day work life.

The central philosophy is that we created the e-mail system, so now we have to manage it. At this point, it seems like electronic mail is managing us, and the results—overload and angst—have become our current legacy. We have the capability and willingness to take control of our e-mails. With this book, you now have the means.

HOW TO READ MANAGING YOUR E-MAIL

This book consists of six chapters:

1. E-mail's Quirks and Wonders: Why e-mail makes us work differently.

2. The Legal Face of E-mail: Navigate the pitfalls and stay out of the courthouse.

3. Using E-mail Judiciously: It's okay to pick up the phone.

4. The Inbox: How to manage your inbox like a pro and reduce e-mail volume in your organization.

5. The Outbox: A guide to good citizenry on the e-mail frontier.

6. The Smoking Gun: Take control and make e-mail work for you.

E-MAIL'S QUIRKS AND WONDERS: Why e-mail makes us work differently.

Chapter 1 opens with the heading "Great Expectations," which frames part of the e-mail problem in terms of our actions and re-actions to using it. We look at the unspoken tensions experienced in the workplace. Debunking e-mail myths gets to the heart of the conundrum between electronic mail as a productivity tool and its overuse eroding the bottom-line, by providing information about the hard numbers and the dollars that are being misspent.

THE LEGAL FACE OF E-MAIL: Navigate the pitfalls and stay out of the courthouse.

Chapter 2 has a strategic focus that delivers a critical set of messages to organizations. Readers will benefit from getting a glimpse of the larger perspectives of e-mail and how all of us can be affected. In this chapter, you learn:

- Why our e-mail messages are so vulnerable
- How e-mail is used in lawsuits, and the costs of not having electronic document retention
- How employees unknowingly contribute to having their e-mails made public
- How departments and organizations can create effective e-mail policies

The focus of the remainder of the book is on specific categories of electronic mail problems. Each chapter outlines stories, problems, research highlights, solutions, and tips. Each chapter provokes thought while inspiring action.

USING E-MAIL JUDICIOUSLY: It's okay to pick up the phone.

Chapter 3 continues the focus on workplace e-mail issues through managing e-mail as a separate communication channel. This discussion leads to a detailed guide to choosing appropriate communication channels to convey information.

In this chapter, you learn:

- When to use e-mail as the appropriate communication channel
- How to avoid the unproductive use of e-mail as a proxy for conversations
- Impacts of corporate culture on employee e-mailing behaviors and perceptions
- Circumstances when the e-mail channel is abused

THE INBOX: How to manage your inbox like a pro and reduce e-mail volume in your organization.

Chapter 4 outlines options for improving control over your inbox and the e-mail system. In this chapter you learn:

- Characteristics of the e-mail volume problem
- Ways to control your inbox for better management
- To identify and control low value messages that clog your inbox
- The problems and solutions regarding group e-mailing and distribution lists
- Features to help you operate your e-mail software
- How to investigate and size-up your e-mail problems

THE OUTBOX: A guide to good citizenry on the e-mail frontier.

Chapter 5 examines the common communication elements that drive our habits in today's workplace. We'll look at time-tested communication principles and show how they apply to e-mail. You learn:

- How to structure an e-mail to deliver high-impact information
- How to write messages that are easily understood
- Best practices for responding to e-mails

THE SMOKING GUN: Take control and make e-mail work for you.

The concluding chapter summarizes some final thoughts on why and how to take control of our inboxes at individual, management, and corporate levels.

There is no doubt that e-mail is an indelible part of our work lives. Technology and electronic mail have brought tremendous benefits to our societies and workplaces. When productivity tools, such as e-mail, that were designed to make our lives easier, turn the tables on us and cause us to work longer hours, making us become further frustrated and isolated from humanity, then it is time for us to regain control.

Fortunately, there is plenty of room for technology and humanity to grow together, productively, and in harmony. I wrote this book with a great deal of personal passion. This passion came from readers like you, who collectively feel that we could do a better job in not only managing our e-mail communications, but all our communications in the workplace. If you follow the guidance offered in this book, you will experience a real sense of both enlightenment and power—enlightenment on the specific causes and effects that promote e-mail's dark side, and the power to take control of this technological Goliath. This power is in your hands now.

CHAPTER 1

E-mail's Quirks and Wonders

E-mail differs from every other form of communication we've ever known. It is direct, global, and usually (but not always) one-to-one, yet it lacks the personal touch of a handwritten letter. Much like television and radio, people often use e-mail to broadcast messages to a wide group of disparate individuals. However, e-mail triggers a response from recipients in a way that broadcast media cannot.

E-mail has had a tremendous impact on our work lives. It is hard to believe that something so inanimate can evoke such strong reactions, as "I love it" or "I hate it." What is it about electronic mail that causes such diverse feelings to surface?

The late communications theorist Marshall McLuhan (1911–1980) predicted e-mail's legacy in the 1960s. He looked for patterns between society and technology advances and believed that each new advance in communication created a shift in the way that we lived, worked, and played. His statement, "We shape the tools and they in turn shape us," was based on observations of how driven and hungry society was becoming to develop new technologies. As our acceptance of electronic mail shows, society was equally ready to embrace them and look for ways to adopt them for our overall pleasure and benefit.

We welcomed e-mail as a productivity tool that would connect us to the world and create new freedoms and efficiencies. It now appears that e-mail is managing the pace of our work, slowing us down in the process through longer, not shorter work hours. In other words, we allow e-mail to dictate too large a part of our work routines. Perhaps it's because e-mail is constantly at work that, more and more, we are as well. This current situation in our workplaces may place us exactly where McLuhan predicted we would be—managing the changes and tensions that new electronic communications impose for our betterment.

Many of us experience a seeming lack of control over electronic mail. We do not use e-mail uniformly. Some thrive on its use, checking their inboxes constantly, while others see e-mail as a low-priority communication channel, checking it infrequently. Most of us are somewhere in between, trying to balance the demands of work and the demands of e-mail.

As with other communication channels at work, use of e-mail has brought about the development of a unique set of usage patterns that color our habits, behaviors, and attitudes toward the device itself. We have developed a love-hate relationship with our favorite communication channel. We have also surrounded e-mail with our perceptions on its purpose and indeed the reason for its very existence. For instance, many people felt that e-mail would signal the end of paper in offices. The reality, as we all know, is quite different. This aspect is covered later in the chapter when we address the many myths about e-mail in the workplace.

E-mail is a fascinating and curious tool. I'm not sure whether it came with its own set of quirks and wonders for us to explore or whether these naturally developed. Regardless, we do find ourselves committing some alarming faux pas when we press the send button. Through my research, I have noted what many respondents have said are the various games people seem to play with electronic mail. This chapter is designed to poke a bit of fun at our fascination with it. We explore some of the commonly held beliefs about e-mail and identify behaviors to make sense of some of the situations we face every day. You may see yourself in these pages, and you will no doubt recognize the patterns that emerge. It is through identifying these patterns that we more deeply understand the sources of our feelings and frustrations with workplace e-mail.

GREAT EXPECTATIONS

Have you ever received a follow-up e-mail or phone call asking if you had received an original e-mail? Or better yet, something I call the "creative" follow-up—a second e-mail that states that you may not have received the first one because of a sender error. E-mail's instantaneous nature has created a set of high expectations in the workplace. This instant scenario is mapped from the impatient sender's perspective in Figure 1.1.

Distribution	Priority	Processing	Response
Instantaneous (Servers being down are no excuse.)	Instantaneous (You are waiting at your computer for an e-mail, aren't you?)	Instantaneous (My request is so brilliantly composed no one could refuse me.)	Instantaneous (It's been 5 minutes; what's taking so long?)

Figure 1.1   Response expectations of impatient e-mail senders.

Most people assume that because many of us have laptop computers, dial-up access at home, and personal digital assistants (PDAs), we should be able to receive and respond to work-based e-mails anytime and anywhere. Such expectations only increase the tension in the communications process. If you tend to think of e-mail simply as a hybrid of written and oral forms of communication, then a typical receiver's expectation for a response follows the pattern shown in Figure 1.2.

According to my research on e-mail management, the majority of us process our incoming mail within 48 hours or sooner, if we know a message is high priority. As we see from Figure 1.2, the time it takes for us to process e-mail messages is not less than it is for written and oral communication because the e-mail medium itself does not affect the amount of consideration that a decision requires. In fact, many of us will

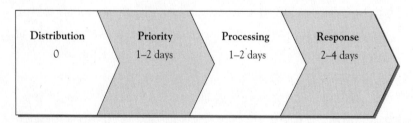

Distribution	Priority	Processing	Response
0	1–2 days	1–2 days	2–4 days

Figure 1.2   Response expectations of a typical e-mail receiver.

deliberately wait to respond to an e-mail message if we want to give an issue greater consideration. Even though e-mail does not directly affect our decision-making process, we feel pressure, both external and internal, to respond to e-mail messages as quickly as possible. E-mail has essentially become *communication without boundaries*.

How do you tend to regard an e-mail about a routine matter that an employee or colleague sends to your work e-mail during the middle of the night or over the weekend? If the sender is traveling across time zones, is preparing to be away from the office (or returning), is simply known at times to be a night owl, or is the CEO, this may not seem unusual.

However, if there are no such circumstances, you might react negatively. You may wonder if the person is trying to impress you or if your colleague is working too hard or is just inefficient. Many executives have told me that while they may review and process e-mail over the weekend, they will not send responses until Monday. We discuss this practice in more detail in Chapter 3.

THE 10 TEMPTATIONS OF E-MAIL

Just as e-mail has caused an unspoken tension in the workplace because of unrealistic expectations for instant response, it has also created and/or magnified other problems, which we discuss next as the 10 temptations of e-mail.

Have you ever noticed how e-mail use, or rather misuse, can bring out the worst in people? This is e-mail's dark side. There are as many cyber sins people commit using e-mail as there are human characteristics; the good news is that I managed to group these offenses into only 10 broad categories. Even better news is that you'll doubtless be able to identify with the 10 temptations I've highlighted, a collection of many behaviors we have seen in others and reactions that we feel during an e-mail stress moment. As you read through the book, you will see these temptations discussed in detail along with solutions for each. For now, view this list as a tidy package designed to compress your collective viewpoints and to encourage better e-mailing habits in all of us.

The Temptation to Send

The tendency to send a message without regard to its significance is based on the mistaken belief that people will read everything that you send and that everything you send is worth reading. It's a sort of narcissistic tendency that only the e-mail communication channel can satisfy. Such e-mail messages can run the gamut from "I loved this, so will you," to multiple copies of the same companywide e-mail, to the cute homilies and kind thoughts for the day, such as "please send to 10 friends, or you will have a bad day." Many of us receive up to a dozen or more of these messages every day and wish we didn't.

The Temptation to Respond

Usually, we just don't know how to respond to these trivial messages. At times, there is an emotional or social need to somehow fill the communication void. Common mistakes include sending a thank you response to acknowledge receipt of the e-mail. It gets worse when the you're welcome e-mail arrives in our inbox. Another common mistake is sending the appreciation e-mail: "Thanks for sending me this information; you can be assured I will give it my full attention." A message like this creates an expectation that at some point you will address the message more fully. It also serves to encourage more sending just to get the response.

The Temptation to Broadcast

At times, this issue defies logical explanation. Distribution lists are a convenient time saver when critical information needs to go to several people. The real problem here is: Which person for which issues? If 10 people from a list of 100 need to receive a message, that is, "send in your forms," why does everyone get it? Or better yet, why are "all employee" e-mails forwarded by some managers with their own direction to read it because it's important? One survey respondent told me: "In Wilmington, I don't need to know that the bathrooms are broken in Minneapolis."

The Temptation to Treat People with Disrespect

This habit can be akin to office tyranny—we send employees an urgent e-mail just to determine how long it takes them to respond or when they are arriving at work. Most of the time, however, this habit relates to a lack of basic politeness in e-mail discourse. There are some people whom you may want to keep at e-mail distance just because of this sort of behavior. However, adding a salutation, such as the recipient's first name, and a closing, such as "Thanks," can significantly change the message's tone. We practice civility in person and over the phone, so why not in e-mail?

The Temptation to React

Even though we can put any type of communication into a text form, this doesn't mean that the message belongs in that form. Some e-mail is composed in such a terse, brusque manner that we tend to react emotionally first, then think about it later. While we are emotionally charged, our fingers are doing the talking over the keyboard, and we triumphantly poke the send button, signifying the "back at you" response. The satisfaction generally lasts 5 to 10 minutes, and then we come to the realization that this might not have been a good idea. Worse yet, we have to undertake face-to-face damage control.

The Temptation to Hide behind E-mail

Have you ever received an apology by e-mail? Have you ever received praise by e-mail? Some employees have actually had their jobs terminated by e-mail. These types of e-mail are simply bad form and tend to expose the sender's reluctance to communicate with us in person. Worse, if the sender is a senior executive, these antics can color our attitudes toward the organization. These types of messages can be a serious catalyst for seeking other employment. It is important to keep in mind that e-mails with negative content can be like bombs—very explosive.

The Temptation toward Mutiny

The sound of a new message arriving puts you into a dilemma: Should you interrupt your work or break your concentration from a meeting or phone call? Do you ever wonder why a colleague or coworker sitting two offices away prefers to send you an e-mail, rather than dropping into your office? Or why someone has suddenly copied you into a set of electronic messages? Again, you are not alone here. These situations all cry out for the human moment when high-touch is preferable to high-tech.

The Temptation to Become Addicted

Some among us prefer e-mail to all other forms of communication. These are people who previously favored memos as their primary form of contact and only used the telephone when absolutely necessary. Voice mail was a godsend for them, because they didn't need to waste their time on banal pleasantries. Some of these users are simply hard-core technology enthusiasts, who become so enamored of their monitors and keyboards that they're mesmerized by them.

Some people attend the meeting, but in reality are simply waiting for the e-mail to arrive. Others see receiving e-mail as a badge of honor and a demonstration of their importance. The cavalier few among us draw attention to themselves by handling their e-mails in public, while commuting on trains and planes. We need to beware of sprouting into technological couch potatoes.

The Temptation to Send Attachments

This one comes straight from the annals of "If you can, do so." At a recent workshop on e-mail, I was asked, "What do you think about receiving an e-mail with 25 attachments?" Luckily I caught myself in time, before responding, "Delete." Somehow people have gotten the crazy notion that while e-mails should be short, attachments are a free-for-all; a bonus gift in which everyone will surely want to share. This is discussed more fully in Myth #6.

The Temptation to Cry Uncle

If there is one message to shout from our office rooftops, it is that it's normal and perfectly acceptable to feel overwhelmed, especially if you are receiving more than the current North American average of 48 e-mails per day. The sense of being swamped becomes more acute as volume increases and reaches almost cosmic proportions at 80 to 100 per day.

Sometimes people feel that it is their fault that they cannot handle or absorb the information, and therefore something must be wrong with them. That is not true—the current e-mail volume is unreasonable and counterproductive. Read on; this book will help!

DEBUNKING E-MAIL MYTHS

Now that we have uncovered some of the idiosyncratic e-mail habits in the workplace, let us dispel some of e-mail's larger-than-life myths.

Myth #1   E-mail Saves Time

Have you ever found yourself sitting at the keyboard in the office and suddenly feeling that you can't type the message you want to send? You are not alone.

Many people experience this phenomenon from time to time—I call it the "keyboard stare"—a sudden state in which your fingers just won't type. Meanwhile, the minutes tick by, and so does your focus on this task and perhaps others. This situation surfaces generally because we want to talk our message rather than type it. We may want to express a number of ideas in a dialogue fashion but unfortunately e-mail seems more convenient. Also, there is no doubt that e-mail provides an invaluable capability to send the same message to many parties, thus saving time spent in separate transmissions. The problem is that now *everyone* gets too many messages, and so we must spend even more time managing our inboxes.

If we quantify the e-mail communication channel in light of the other three—face-to-face, telephone, and paper-based—then e-mail represents a 33 percent increase in communication opportunity. If e-mail simply off-loaded communication traffic from the other three channels, there would be fewer meetings, fewer telephone calls, and fewer paper-based items—the slack having been taken up by electronic mail. But this has not happened.

E-mail has not dramatically impacted message complexities and symbolic meanings, only the corporate context. So we have ramped up its use because the capacity exists, without relinquishing our need for the use of the other channels. The result has been a lengthening of the work day, estimated at an hour per day (to be explored in more detail in Myth #2).

Executives who proactively manage their department's e-mails report receiving an average of 25 per day—a figure they believe is realistic and manageable. Comparing this to the current average of 48 a day, we have almost doubled the volume of necessary e-mails. We can therefore conclude that people who are receiving more than 25 e-mails every day are probably:

- Receiving more information than they need
- Receiving more information than they can read
- Working longer days just to manage the excess traffic

Ask 10 people if they would give up their e-mail system and most would probably say "absolutely not." We cannot imagine working without e-mail, nor should we have to. E-mail clearly has an opportunity cost, but at 25 messages per day, the benefits of this communication channel far outweigh the cost. At 40 or more messages per day, the productivity costs become marginal.

One last word on the myth of e-mail productivity: Have you ever been speaking to a person on the telephone when he or she suddenly asks you to repeat what you just said? If so, you can probably safely assume that they are probably trying to knock off a few e-mails while conversing with you. While this may seem a noble effort to multitask when time is scarce, it actually reduces productivity. Why? Because the phone call takes longer for both parties while key points are repeated. In addition, the e-mails require full concentration if they are to be effective communication devices. So instead of multitasking for efficiency, we are actually creating more unnecessary work. We discuss this more in Chapter 5.

Myth #2   Using E-mail Is Profitable

"Tell me what you like best about e-mail?"

A popular response to this survey question is that e-mail allows the same message to be transmitted to several individuals simultaneously. The implication is that e-mail provides tangible efficiency and an overt cost savings (e.g., "Without e-mail, when would I have the time to pass this information to my direct reports?").

"Tell me what you like least about e-mail?"

"There is too much," is the common lament. The implication is that e-mail carries with it user burdens that equate to personal or sweat equity, which many tend to consider nontangible (e.g., I now have to borrow from my personal time to keep up).

Does e-mail have a cost? Are you always better off using e-mail? At what point (if any) does using e-mail become an opportunity loss? How much e-mail is too much?

Calculating E-mail's Demands on Our Time

My research shows that 64 percent of e-mail messages require a response. Using that number, we can derive the following characteristics for workplace e-mail:

1. 64 percent of e-mail requires a response—5 minutes spent on average for each response.
2. 36 percent of e-mail doesn't require a response and can be divided into two groups:
   a. 50 percent are of low or no relevance—2 minutes to consider and delete each item.
   b. 50 percent are for information only—8 minutes to deal with each item (whether to read, to file and read later, or to skim and discard).

Using the natural rate of 25 e-mails (established in Myth #1), we can calculate the amount of time spent on e-mail, as follows:

16 e-mails require response at 5 minutes each = 80 minutes

5 e-mails are irrelevant at 2 minutes each = 10 minutes

4 e-mails for info only at 8 minutes each = 32 minutes

= 122 minutes

Because most of us receive approximately 48 e-mails a day, we can now recalculate the total time we spend managing e-mail during a typical workday as shown in Table 1.1.

To keep these estimates as conservative as possible, let's assume that you process information more quickly than the average person either because you are a quick typist or because you keep your responses to e-mail as brief as possible. Reducing the processing times by 25 percent still results in three hours a day spent managing e-mail.

Earlier, I said that it takes the average worker about two hours a day to manage 25 messages. Therefore, we can compute the minimum daily overload that e-mail is causing each day as shown in Table 1.2.

Table 1.1 Daily Time Spent Managing Average E-mail Volumes

48 E-mails per Day	Number of E-mails	Time in Minutes
Response required (64%)	31	155
Irrelevant (18%)	9	18
Information only (18%)	8	64
Total	48	237
		3.95 hours

Table 1.2 E-mail Overload: Daily Calculation Based on Average E-mail Volumes

48 E-mails per Day	Time (Hours)
Total time spent	3.95
Above reduced by 25%	2.96
Less: time spent on 25 e-mails per day	2.03
E-mail overload per day	0.93

Now let's consider a situation that we've all faced—dealing with e-mail messages after we've spent time away from the office. How do these calculations look when we are faced with 200 e-mail messages?

The numbers in Table 1.3 illustrate how much time we spend on e-mails that require a response, coupled with the time it takes for us to wade through irrelevant and low-level information. And let's not forget the time it takes for us to figure out how to tackle this huge mess.

The greatest levels of dissatisfaction with the e-mail channel relate to the sheer volume of messages we receive in our

Table 1.3 Time Spent Processing 200 E-mails

200 New E-mails	Number of E-mails	Time (Minutes)	Time (Hours)
Response required (64%)	128	640	10.7
Irrelevant (18%)	36	72	1.2
Information only (18%)	36	288	4.8
Total	200	1,000	16.7

inboxes. In particular, it's the volume of unnecessary messages that aggravate most of us because it's so easy for people to send us information. Irrelevant or low-priority e-mail traffic not only impedes our ability to prioritize our inboxes, it also dampens our motivation to do so.

The costs of stress-related factors are difficult to capture, and I have ignored them in my calculations. However, we must nevertheless make allowances for them. Depending on your industry and organization, the allowances could easily be an additional 20 percent.

Now that we have dealt with e-mail's intangible costs, what about the potential impact of its more tangible costs? Our calculations of e-mail overload can help here.

Let's make the following assumptions:

Employee annual salary	$50,000
Cost of benefits (25 percent)	$12,500
Fully loaded corporate cost	$62,500 per annum
Hourly employee cost (260 days at 7.5 hours per)	$32.05

The annual cost per employee of e-mail overload (still using our conservative figures) is shown in Table 1.4.

The more e-mails we receive each day, the more these costs increase, with the most costly shift occurring between 48 and 75 e-mails a day. Again, these are tangible costs, and do not include the intangible (and indeterminate) costs that stress has on our productivity and motivation.

These numbers may appear relative and simply the cost of doing business. Some skeptics may argue that a saving of a few

Table 1.4 Calculation of Annual Cost of E-mail Overload per Employee

E-mails	National Average (2002)	High-Volume Average
Number of e-mails	48	75
E-mail overload per day	0.93 hours	2.62 hours
Hourly employee cost	$32.05	$32.05
E-mail overload cost per year per employee	$7,750	$21,830

thousand dollars per year for each employee, if that employee was not coping with wasteful, low-value e-mail, would be wasted somewhere else. So why bother to be concerned? After all, virtually all employees use e-mail in the workplace, and no one today would ever do without it.

But for an entrepreneur with 100 employees, this equates to an annual cost of nearly $250,000 (assuming the average number of messages these employees receive is 35 a day). Ask these entrepreneurs if they would like to find an easy way to save $250,000 in operating costs every year and they will surely jump at the chance. What about larger organizations that employ thousands of people? For every 1,000 employees who earn an average of $50,000 a year and receive approximately 48 messages a day, there is potentially $7.7 million every year that is wasted on excess, low-value e-mail traffic.

If these same employees receive 75+ e-mails per day, then the annual cost can jump to over $21 million. Again, these are purposely conservative calculations that show most companies' real costs. These numbers are based on an annual salary of $70,000. What happens to the costs for employees earning $150,000 who receive 75 e-mails a day? In this case, it would take only 179 of these executive employees to create an e-mail overload cost of $12 million. Factor in the effects stress has on motivation and productivity, and this is definitely money that is spent to achieve negative returns.

Although e-mail is a productivity tool, it is also a critical corporate resource that requires the attention of line managers and executives to ensure its most cost effective operation.

Myth #3   E-mail Expands Communication Flow

E-mail has become the most dominant form of communication in the workplace, virtually rendering the business memo or facsimile extinct, while minimizing varying levels of personal contact. Electronic mail capability in the workplace has created the following assumptions:

- E-mail has brought back the art of written communication.
- E-mail communication carries unexpected emotional weight.
- Access to e-mail destroys communication barriers, thereby creating workplace democracy.
- Many e-mail users don't consider privacy an issue.

Let's review each of these assumptions.

The Art of Written Communication

Electronic mail has definitely brought back the art of written communication, but clear, concise writing is a skill that is challenging for many people. Whether you have seen the world's longest e-mail (the paragraph that never ends) or the world's shortest e-mail (a one-letter response such as Y, N, or OK), I am sure that you are all too familiar with the challenges of message composition in the workplace.

Writing weaknesses abound. I recall receiving an e-mail from an author who had written several books—what he had to relate impressed me very much. I then forwarded this message to a friend who was a fan of the author. His response? A curt e-mail that noted that the author should learn how to spell. Admittedly, I was angry with my friend for being so critical, but the impression remained. The written word really does matter.

Although e-mail is the quickest way to share written forms of communication, it may not be the quickest way to create a mutual understanding. I am sure you can easily recall e-mail messages that caused you alarm, concern, or anger, yet most of them weren't sent with that intention. Do you remember the first angry message you received or the most recent? What about messages that you sent prematurely?

Emotional Weight

While e-mail can be seen as information with motion, it is also information with *emotion*. In the absence of the barriers of time, distance, and editing for composition and tone, e-mail messages are a very direct route from one person's thoughts to another. Therefore, electronic messages carry an emotional weight. It is this emotional weight that many e-mail users in a workplace setting have underestimated.

Too often, we send messages that we should deliver in person. Unfortunately, the e-mail channel makes it easy for us to say things that we would never say directly to a person, making it easy for us to "hide." In the workplace, we need to enhance our communication by ensuring that we use e-mail only when it's appropriate and not by default. We must keep the other channels of communication open for use as well.

Destroying Communication Barriers

Another often-heralded benefit of e-mail is its ability to connect all users and virtually transcend hierarchies. Rather than sending letters to your government representative, which you would expect to be intercepted by an aide, you now have the power to reach your representative by e-mail. Not true, since most elected representatives have their aides respond to your e-mail messages. The CEO of a Fortune 500 corporation may see your e-mail but it's just as likely that an executive assistant may handle it. Although you can use e-mail to reach the offices of the powerful, your message may have no more impact than a letter would have had 10 years ago. Some cyber buffs may have regarded e-mail as the key to global connectivity, world peace, and environmental harmony; the truth is that electronic mail is just another communication channel with its own limitations.

E-mail Privacy

In today's electronic age, most of us have concluded that all things digital, monitored, and stored have replaced human contact. We suspect that we have another boss—one who lurks within the bowels of our computer and its e-mail system and is watching our every move. Some companies, in an effort to discourage personal e-mails, tell workers that their "e-mail may be monitored."

Most of us are familiar with the highly publicized corporate lawsuits that center on crucial e-mail messages. Batteries of lawyers examining e-mail messages retrieved from executive offices and assessing their context—what were the messages really conveying? Was there more than one meaning? How far from the actual truth can we push the envelope to make these words and sentences fit our side of the case?

Should we care about privacy while using our workplace e-mail systems? Some of us may argue that controlling e-mail messaging restricts the free flow of information that it was intended to unleash. Again, there is not one simple answer, but trends can be quite revealing. Few people today would use e-mail to convey formative corporate strategies. In their view, verbal discussions and informal note-taking afford the best protection to sensitive corporate information.

Myth #4   E-mail Creates a Paperless Office

Does part of our drive to use e-mail come from the notion that we are working toward a paperless office?

For decades we have been hearing about the cashless society and the paperless office. It appears that technology prognosticators made these predictions much too soon. According to the book, *The Myth of the Paperless Office,* we are not ready to forgo paper for thinking or processing information because paper helps us to concentrate on new ideas and complex tasks. It stimulates both the creative and the collaborative processes.

While technology has given us the ability in many instances to work without paper, some tasks are best done on paper. For instance, I could never imagine the late John Lennon or George Harrison composing lyrics on a laptop while sitting in an airport—could you? Collaborative composition cannot be fully effected through technology. During corporate America's darker days in 2001 to 2002, paper shredders were center-stage as companies tried to destroy written documents to keep ahead of litigation. This is a current testament to our human and legitimate reliance on paper. Of course, we now know that they should have been equally concerned about destroying their hard drives that retained so many of their "deleted" electronic messages!

Quite simply, there are not many paperless offices in existence because we don't consider paper passé. Rather, the introduction of electronic messages has simply provided another option for recording and storing information. E-mail was not designed to create the paperless office any more than debit cards were intended to replace currency. They are alternatives that serve to enhance and expand on basic capabilities. What the advent of e-mail has generated is, in fact, a greater need and dependence on paper.

Using e-mail to send and receive messages has simply changed when and how we introduce paper into our information-gathering repertoire. For example, prior to e-mail, we received most information via paper. We dealt with the paper, making notes and comments, and then either returned the documents (after making copies for files) or filed the items directly.

In an e-mail system, we receive information principally via monitors. From a process of elimination, we can make the following estimates about the nature of workplace e-mail: Some information (up to 20 percent) we read and quickly acknowledge by return e-mail or no response is required. Another 20 percent of e-mail is workplace spam from a variety of sources (we discuss this later). Another 20 percent is internally generated corporate communication from a variety of senior executives and/or functional departments. The remaining 40 percent is more complex and requires printing, collating, reading, and filing, just like the days before e-mail.

So if you're receiving 50 e-mails per day, you will print approximately 20 of them along with their attachments. This assessment correlates quite closely with the aforementioned book's estimates that office e-mail increases paper consumption by 40 percent each year. Still not convinced? Then consider these statistics:

- North American paper consumption per capita increased by 12 percent from 1989 to 1999.
- The use of uncoated free-sheet paper (used in photocopiers, printers, and facsimile machines) increased in the United States by 14 percent between 1995 and 2000.

- Experts have tabulated that North American office printers spewed out 1.2 trillion sheets of paper in 2001; an increase of 50 percent since 1996.

Myth #5   All IT Professionals Are E-mail Efficiency Experts

Not all e-mail problems are the exclusive domain of an organization's IT personnel, who are regularly called on to resolve e-mail overload issues. IT professionals are there to ensure that systems are available for continued, unfettered, uninterrupted use. Their responsibilities are vast and complex, but relate largely to the mechanics of the operating systems and infrastructures that support the "front end" of organizations. Their concerns center on features such as efficiency of information flow, system capacity, integration of multiple systems, and technological architecture.

Given such a well-defined scope of operation, why is it that we turn to our IT experts to resolve end-user e-mail issues and problems?

I often use the analogy of another technologically-based communication channel—the telephone. For example, if you don't have a dial tone, you would call the internal phone support group or the phone company. However, if one of your employees is spending too much time on the telephone each work day or is making repeated annoying calls to certain individuals, would you, as the manager, call the phone company? No, this would clearly be an employee-management issue, and you would deal with it accordingly.

E-mail, as another technology-based communication channel, is no different. Problems with being able to send and receive e-mails, like the telephone's dial tone, are the domain of the IT professional. Problems with getting too many e-mails from unwanted and/or well-intentioned sources are not—these are problems for management to resolve.

Myth #6   Attachments Don't Require Management

When I wrote my research study in 2001, I made the 30-page report available in both paper and electronic formats. I also developed a three-page executive summary, which reduced the complex information to its most critical elements.

Whenever I get a request for an electronic copy of this report, I always offer the three-page executive summary first. After the recipients have had a chance to review it, I then state that if they still want the entire report (and I indicate clearly that it is 30 pages, low graphics), then I'm happy to pass it along electronically. This scenario is what I call "attachments management."

Do e-mail attachments require management? Just ask the number of remote users who often need to press the "CTRL-ALT-DEL" sequence to stop the loading operation. Or ask the executive who receives a 30-slide PowerPoint document along with accompanying notes the night before your presentation. Some senders treat attachments like tiny electronic bits that show up on the e-mail message template as a colored icon. For many receivers they are explosive, expanding jack-in-the-boxes, ready to jump out at you at a mere click and bury you in information. Some people view attachments as a freebie—"Yes, I kept my e-mail short, well-tailored, and to the point." Then the attachment demon takes hold and a 10-page report pops up.

We need to treat attachments like any other communication, all the while keeping bandwidth capability in mind. After all, one of the many great things about e-mail is its portability—you can log on at an Internet Café in Kuala Lumpur just as easily as powering up your laptop on a Caribbean beach. That's why it's important that we manage our attachments in an effort to consider the location of our receiver. We also need to manage attachments for their size. How big is too big? Many people, especially remote users, will say that 5MB is too large. Others will say that they don't need all the graphics to make an assessment or to have the basic text information prior to seeing a live presentation. Still others will lament that they don't want to see 30-page draft reports.

Once again, the fact that we can send a 30-page report doesn't automatically mean that we should. If we must, then we should highlight the sections that require closer scrutiny. We probably would have instinctively done this with a hard copy report, yet when we are using technology as the transmission channel, we seem to abandon the reviewer preparations.

Another related issue is the attachment *headcount*—how many attachments are you sending and why? Again, even though technology permits us to send 20 or 30 separate attachments, why do so? In other words, send attachments only when absolutely necessary. If you want to send two attachments, think twice about whether the information is expected and/or welcome.

Let's look at this from another angle. How do you feel when you open an e-mail message and see five, six, or more attachment icons pop up? Happy that someone was thinking of your best interests, or annoyed that someone is pushing more work in your direction?

Myth #7   There Is Nothing We Can Do about Managing E-mail

Here is an interesting myth. Managing our inboxes is definitely possible and completely within our grasp. Although we seem to have less direct control over the messages we receive in our inbox—they appear and we react—technological applications such as filters do allow us to have some control over their ultimate destination. For example, we can choose to direct some messages to folders and delete others. We can also start sending fewer messages. It's like the old adage, the fewer we send the fewer we will receive. So far, this may seem easier said than done, but the next couple of chapters in the book will give so many reasons why we shouldn't choose to send e-mail that this myth may start to fade.

So for now, remember that the messages we do choose to send are completely within our control and are an excellent place to start taking some personal action. If we have the knowledge and the tools to help us recognize the types of problems that can occur with our e-mail communications, then we can begin to make changes for the better. Perhaps our exemplary messages to others will establish a new paradigm for them to follow.

INSTANT MESSAGING

Our discussions on e-mail's quirks and wonders would not be complete without acknowledging electronic communication's kid brother—the instant message. IM, as it is commonly known, started in the late 1990s to provide online, real time access among users on a "buddy list." Compiled and managed by each IM user, the buddy list shows who is actually online at any given time, and therefore available as a potential conversational partner. The "conversations" are of course text-based and to date have been the nearest thing to synchronous electronic communication. IM, like e-mail, got its start at home through free public systems offered by major Internet service providers. IM, like e-mail, has found its way into the workplace. Unlike e-mail, most IM use is not supported through corporate platforms.

But this too is starting to change as both compatible software and corporate interest in IM begins to take hold. Since 2002, Wall Street has had a growing love affair with IM as a method to transmit quick (and secure) messages within its institutional walls and among its client base. IM is making its way into the workplace at exponential rates to satisfy a need to stay connected, but on a less formal basis. The growth of IM seems to be an unconscious recognition of the limitations of e-mail communication for casual, quick, and informal bantering that is such a necessary part of our organizational work life.

Let's take a brief look at communication systems within organizations. There are two basic systems:

1. *Formal.* Structured communication, usually prepared in advance, conveying some form of authority.

2. *Informal.* Casual, relaxed communication that emphasizes personal knowledge and common bonds.

These systems can move in three directions within organizations: upward (to superiors), across (to colleagues), and downward (to subordinates). The direction of communication affects both the style of the communication and the expectations of the receiver(s):

Direction	Expected Communication Style
Upward	Organized, logical, respecting hierarchies
Across	More personable with an emphasis on collegiality and common purpose
Downward	Information organized to suit the work group, the communication style is friendly yet professional

While the above dimensions are directly applicable to the formal communication system, they can also be applied to informal communication. We still observe greater formality in uncertain workplace situations, perhaps because workplace cultures continue to reinforce these communication rituals. Yet, our richest sources of information in the workplace tend to come from informal sources.

Henry Mintzberg first proved this in his book *The Nature of Managerial Work.* His studies on exchange of workplace information showed clearly that managers and executives rely heavily on informal communication systems to glean what he termed "soft information." A common term used for many informal communication exchanges is "the grapevine."

Some people think of the grapevine as simply hearsay and low-level office gossip, but it is a most powerful tool for the transmission of information that affects people within organizations. Although e-mail has the capability to spread information to multiple parties, the grapevine has the power to move information at Internet-like speeds. E-mail is definitely not the preferred mechanism for transmission of this type of informal information because it is too impersonal and lacks privacy. Exchanges of grapevine information are like a critical social glue that binds the workplace together. It is emotive and requires our expectations of instant human feedback to make the exchange complete.

For example:

DAVID: "There's a rumor going around that Brian is about to be sacked."

PERSON NO. 1: "Really? I'll believe it when I see it."

PERSON NO. 2: "Oh, that's too bad. I like working with him."

PERSON NO. 3: "Fantastic—that is the best news I've heard in a long time. How do you know?"

We can see here a variety of reactions. The information has been accepted for its potential as truth and also for its delicious speculation value. There is also a sense of community and belonging that we feel when someone trusts us enough to let us into their risky and intimate ideas. This is informal information power at its best. While there is a perception that grapevine information is inaccurate, studies show it is not only largely legitimate but 80 percent accurate.

In this example of a face-to-face verbal exchange, we can see and feel the value of tantalizing workplace speculation. We can also see that this effect would be dampened, if not completely lost through using e-mail. Now imagine this scenario playing out through IM and you can see that the same tantalizing impact returns, because of the intimacy and immediacy of the medium itself. This helps to explain why IM is being self-installed on thousands of workplace computers each week.

It's interesting to start to draw some parallels between IM and e-mail's entry to the workplace. When e-mail was formally introduced and supported by corporations, its role was somewhat confused. Workers had questions because of e-mail's roots as home-based communication. Was it part of the formal communication system or of the informal? Now that I have access to everyone by e-mail, can I use this communication with senior executives? Electronic mail is not like a memorandum; do I really need to compose one, or can I just let it rip as it comes out of my thoughts?

Matters of content involving organizing thoughts, structure, clarity, and grammar remain the trademark of communication expressed in text form. We know that the easiest way to have your e-mail message judged poorly is to lapse into lazy writing habits that create negative impressions. With IM, this pressure is released and we can communicate in abbreviations, acronyms, and short phrases without observing any formal style at all.

Studies on IM in the workplace suggest that use of this electronic subchannel is informal and like the grapevine, mainly focused on work-related activities. Another parallel to the grapevine is the transitory nature of these conversations—short bursts of information and reactions back and forth, where participants are easily able to switch to more formal matters. An additional feature of IM is its "time out" capability. With IM, you aren't expected to focus your full attention on these conversations, and they are intermittent enough that they can easily slide into those quick mental breaks that we take from even the most exciting and grueling work. IM truly acts like that social glue among coworkers.

IM also acts like a bridge between the other interactive communication channels. People will use it to check on whether their coworkers are available for an impromptu face-to-face chat or switch out of it to the telephone if the content of their messages requires more dialogue. There is rarely any channel switching between IM and e-mail. The reason is that IM is the electronic version of a casual conversation, not a transmission of information.

This chapter provided an introduction to the myriad of e-mail issues that swirl around us in our workplaces. This information is the foundation that prepares you to get the most out of the rest of this book. The observations offered here are designed to be digestible and thought provoking. They are also designed to give you clues on the breadth of issues that we all face in our collective struggles with e-mail. We can't begin to solve the problems until we have an understanding of their basic nature and their impacts both in terms of time and cost.

This chapter frames your perspectives on e-mail to motivate meaningful changes—both large and small—on your daily use and indeed, the choices you make when using e-mail. The next chapter guides you through the many hidden issues you face with your e-mails when considered from a legal viewpoint.

CHAPTER 2

The Legal
Face of E-mail

The first publicized case in which e-mail was used as evidence was the Iran-Contra scandal involving the White House and Lt. Col. Oliver North. During the mid-1980s investigation on the nature of the U.S. military's role in Nicaragua, Oliver North became the administration's messenger. The investigators were dissatisfied with the information that Lt. Col. North offered because it ostensibly denied any legitimate military involvement with the Contras. The hearings and the sensational media coverage dragged on until the fateful day when Lt. Col. North's testimony changed direction and the matter was quickly concluded. The Central Intelligence Agency investigation discovered that not only had the military used e-mail messages to convey critical information, but that backup tapes of the messages existed in the White House. In 1985, these high-profile correspondents never suspected that their communications would be anything but strictly confidential and have the highest levels of security clearances. It isn't difficult to understand the reason for Lt. Col. North's sudden change in his testimony—the written word, when properly referenced, sourced, and verified, cannot be easily refuted.

In the past few years, there has been extensive coverage in the news media about lawyers and regulators subpoenaing e-mail messages. The subjects of e-mails have made news headlines. We take great interest in reading excerpts from e-mail messages that are printed verbatim for the general public's scrutiny.

While most people realize that their workplace e-mail is not private, they seem to think that the issue doesn't affect them. "Why would anyone want to read my e-mails?" they wonder, "I haven't done anything illegal." Do these assumptions sound familiar? Judging from our exposure to these issues solely through media coverage, it stands to reason that only those committing crimes in large companies should be concerned with the legal face of e-mail.

However, what if you are working on a competitive or industry-sensitive issue? Have you ever considered that other people could scrutinize the information you commit to e-mail and use it to support a lawsuit against you or your company? For instance, what if you work for a midsized regional firm, you manage people, and there is a job performance issue. As the supervisor, would you freely use e-mail to document your decisions and directives if you thought these might become part of a legal case against your company? Now that e-mail is such a well-known communication channel, employees and companies contemplate more legal actions each day because of the certainty that electronic evidence exists.

This chapter provides you with an awareness and understanding of the potential for our workplace e-mails to play a role in the legal arena. First we discuss the causes of e-mail-driven litigation and possible preventative measures, including:

- Why corporate e-mail messages are so vulnerable
- Where messages can be intercepted
- How e-mail messages can be used as legal evidence (under what circumstances e-mails become smoking guns)

Once we come to understand how and why e-mail can be used against us in court, we'll explore preventative measures that can limit our liability. Step by step, we'll address:

- Individual actions
- Formulating an organization's e-mail guidelines
- Developing an organization's e-mail retention policy

The concepts and information presented in this chapter should be considered a basic blueprint. As in Chapter 1, we will attempt to debunk some commonly held myths about e-mail's legal face. Our purpose is to further enlighten you on the hidden traps and treasures of e-mail.

WHY OUR E-MAIL MESSAGES ARE SO VULNERABLE

A word that is often used in articles about workplace e-mail is *ephemeral*—the mistaken notion that e-mails "live" for only a few days; that e-mail messages are transitory and never permanent. We have fooled ourselves into regarding our e-mail correspondence as we would a conversation—a surrogate for a more personal exchange like the telephone or face-to-face. It is this misconception about e-mail that is potentially dangerous.

Question: What is an e-mail's shelf life?

   a. Short—when I delete it, it is gone.
   b. My company has an expunge policy and they delete e-mail records periodically.
   c. For as long as the e-mail resides on either the sender's or receiver's personal computer, either in folders or the inbox.
   d. Potentially indefinite.

If you picked (b) and you are not a technology professional, I would say that your knowledge of your firm's e-mail system and its policies on retaining e-mail documents is well above average. Nevertheless, this does not account for *both* the sender and receiver. The correct answer is (d). The remaining answers, as we shall see in the following section, are dangerous misconceptions.

You should never underestimate how vulnerable you are as originators of e-mail. You have no control over your recipients' decisions to forward your messages to others without your knowledge or consent. Indeed, the recipient has many personal options available for prolonging the life of an e-mail message. For example, the message can be forwarded not once, but countless times, and those recipients in turn can retain it for their own purposes—by downloading, saving on numerous drives, and printing—all of this without your being aware of it. The irony in comparing paper to electronic communication is that paper records can be destroyed, leaving little trace of their existence. E-mail records live on indefinitely and can always be traced from numerous sources. In this context, it appears that paper-based messages are ephemeral, while e-mail messages are eternal. But it's even more interesting than that.

We now commit a broader range of casual and corporate cultural information to institutional memory, and because we tend to compose e-mail messages as we would speak them, we often create a content-rich environment that can come under future scrutiny. In the days before e-mail, before most information exchanges were committed to writing, *plausible deniability* was still a claim that people could use to represent (or intentionally misrepresent) an unpleasant workplace situation. Plausible deniability is similar to the "he said, she said," argument—the truth is usually found somewhere in the middle, unless, as in the Iran-Contra scandal and countless others, one of the parties has irrefutable evidence. In that case, the balance of power tips in favor of the evidence and settlements usually follow.

Before e-mail achieved its popularity in the mid-1990s, interoffice memoranda served as the fundamental mode to capture the corporate written word. Invariably, a process that generally involved much consideration, preparation, editing, and approval within the department prior to final signoff and distribution surrounded this type of documentation. Was there an inherent rationale for what organizations chose to commit to paper and the care that they took to prepare it? The advent of personal computers on every desk definitely signaled that internal processes were speeding up. This characteristic of personal computers carried with it the notion that e-mail communication was the most convenient way to quickly relay messages and ideas to others. The careful preparation and consideration that was reserved for written memorandums fell by the wayside.

As a result, we often have an all-too-casual approach to the content of our e-mail correspondence. Because we have our own computer on our desks, this seems to reinforce our assumption that everything we type into that device is private. E-mail gives us false confidence about writing things that we normally might never have committed to paper. It is this aspect that becomes so interesting to lawyers and so potentially damaging to our organizations and to us.

As early as 1992, a Boston-based legal consulting firm aptly likened e-mail to a corporate citizens band (CB) radio. "It is full of corporate gossip, and derogatory or indiscreet remarks. It paints a very down-to-earth picture of corporate knowledge and behavior. And it is meticulously transcribed and stored."*

---

*Martha Middleton, "A Discovery: There May Be Gold in E-mail," *National Law Journal*, 16 (September 20, 1993).

Stories abound about companies that have been caught in this type of web. For example:

1. A New York-based company filed suit against another company over what they suspected was a fraudulent sale of corporate assets. The suing company alleged that e-mail messages from the selling company would support their claim. During the investigation of computer records, e-mails were found that gave opinions on the draft agreements then in preparation. Comments mentioned disguising information to avoid antitrust violations. This evidence was enough to force a quick, yet embarrassing settlement. The selling company was then further investigated at great additional costs to themselves.

2. A California-based firm sued a rival who claimed that a former executive shared trade secrets by e-mail. It took a legal team six weeks to pore over nearly 900 e-mail accounts looking for supporting evidence. Deleted computer files were also requested—this was a more complex search because many hard drive files were over-written leaving only fragments to work from. However, forensic computer experts have come a long way and enough electronic information was found not only in support of the original allegation, but also on the sued company's cavalier attitude toward fair business practices. As a result, this company faced both criminal and civil actions. In the final outcome, the company was threatened with bankruptcy and another firm purchased their assets.

Never before has more information existed that we can access via legal channels—and access is just the start. As we have seen from these examples, producing e-mail records and other computer-related documentation is time consuming and expensive. Lawyers and forensics experts can easily spend hundreds of hours sifting through electronic information to determine what information is truly relevant to their case. All too often a legal team, for discovery purposes, will request *all* e-mails that are generated within an organization between two specific dates because there is no other way for third parties to independently arrive at the electronic story that best supports their clients' perspective and allegations. Given the massive volumes of the electronic data that can be generated by mid- to large-size firms each day, attempting to discover documents over a three- to four-month period of corporate activity can translate to tens of thousands of documents and hundreds of hours of investigation.

Electronic-discovery software enables lawyers to search documents by keywords and sort them into more manageable categories for examination. An example of the time and cost savings that electronic-discovery tools can provide comes from a recent situation in New England where 20,000 pages of e-mail required discovery. The manual price tag was estimated at $6 million, while the electronic search solution was estimated at $500,000.

We can only imagine how much the 2002 Wall Street investment bank investigations may have actually cost. It is also no surprise that some of these banking departments have placed a moratorium on e-mail use, stating that either nothing but confirmation of instructions or routine requests be made electronically, and that all other messages must be communicated via a written memorandum. This may be too drastic a solution, but we can see how we need to become more mindful about using e-mail in the course of our business dealings.

Let's take another look at what is now becoming an all too familiar story: In 2001, a Fortune 500 company was involved in a wrongful termination lawsuit. All company records relating to this employee's termination were subpoenaed, including e-mails. The company's lawyers met with the IT department to begin the process of sorting through the records. What they discovered was that it would be impossible for the IT department to sort through the millions of e-mail records that the company generated over the requested four-month period. With this knowledge, the company applied to the court for relief on producing the e-mail records, because they were not stored in a manner that made them easily accessible. The court refused, citing that document and record maintenance was the company's responsibility.

There was a solution but it was not a pretty one. Almost one million company e-mail records for the four months in question were printed out. Representatives of the legal team had to carefully examine each e-mail record just to find those records that pertained to the lawsuit. No firm wants its corporate laundry aired publicly, especially through the mouths of a legal team. Worse yet, this exercise cost the company $750,000, and the legal team didn't find anything within the e-mails that assisted either party in the case. Ultimately, the company settled with the plaintiff. So not only were they out-of-pocket on the settlement, they were significantly out-of-pocket as a result of the e-mail search.

E-mail retention becomes a much larger issue when mixed with the potency of a lawsuit. Many organizations are learning the hard way that their assumptions about record retention were wrong. As with so many of our process enhancements, the basic problem here is that organizations do not take thinking and planning far enough. Companies are over-taxed with more initiatives than time or money permits. No doubt, many companies assume that if it is electronic, searching and sorting capabilities will be equally pain-free.

More lawyers are aware of this situation and now almost automatically default to requesting e-mail records as part of their discovery process. Many companies do not purge any of their records, let alone their e-mail records, and often it is within the text of materials that are considered old or have already been archived that lawyers find their "smoking guns." Furthermore, the fact that lawyers are able to examine thousands of a company's e-mails often results in public revelations about how the company handles other issues—some of them sensitive—within its overall corporate culture. As we saw in our first two examples, these disclosures can be equally damaging in a court of law.

At this point, you may be asking yourself what is e-mail retention and why should I care about it? Even though the high-profile discoveries in large corporations or government receive the media attention, the problem is widespread. A little bit of knowledge in this area is worthwhile and may stimulate further consideration and dialog within organizations to ensure that e-mail records become part of their overall document retention strategy. This will be covered later in the chapter.

WHERE MESSAGES CAN BE INTERCEPTED

*Question: At how many points can an e-mail message
be intercepted?*

a. None

b. Two—the sender's outbox and the receiver's inbox

c. One—my company's corporate server

d. Four—Two corporate servers and their backup tapes

e. Almost infinite

If you chose answers (d) or (e) then you are definitely on the right track. Earlier we addressed why third parties may read your e-mail messages and the difficulties companies face in trying to produce them. By now you are aware that using workplace e-mail is akin to laying your soul bare for anyone in the world to see. The good news is that because so many millions of e-mail messages are sent each day, the effort required to retrieve and to read the messages are time and cost prohibitive, unless there is a good reason. When I think of e-mail's darker side, I am reminded of Marshall McLuhan's statement, "The content of any new media blinds us to its character." It's time for us to take a closer look at e-mail's dark side.

The risks inherent in writing e-mail messages are:

- They can be read out of context and at face value.

- They can be monitored by those to whom they are not directed.

- They can be forwarded or intercepted without our knowledge.

To understand how an e-mail message can become public information, Figure 2.1 traces the typical route your e-mail takes within the corporate environment. You initiate the message from your inbox and it is routed to an e-mail server, which finds the receiver's address and directs the message to that inbox. So far, this process resembles the traditional postal delivery service, where your letter is sent, sorted, and delivered to your home. The differences with an e-mail system are the speed at which the message is handled and the server's backup capabilities. Every item that passes through the e-mail server is copied and saved on the backup. The primary purpose of the backup is to provide a fail-safe if the e-mail server is off-line or otherwise inoperative.

Backup tapes and drives have enormous capacity and they are generally the source for subpoenaed e-mails. Figure 2.1 illustrates e-mail routing at its simplest level. Within larger companies, there may be multiple e-mail servers, in which case the message would flow from server to server until it could be posted to the receiver's inbox. With each server it passes through, the e-mail is copied to that server's backup. Figure 2.2 shows another typical example.

In this diagram, an e-mail message is liberally exposed because it touches many points in transit. It starts from your inbox and routes through the e-mail server after being copied by the server's backup. Then the e-mail is cast adrift over the Internet while company server A attempts to link with company server B. As it passes through the Internet, the e-mail can

Figure 2.1   Typical route for e-mail using a shared corporate server.

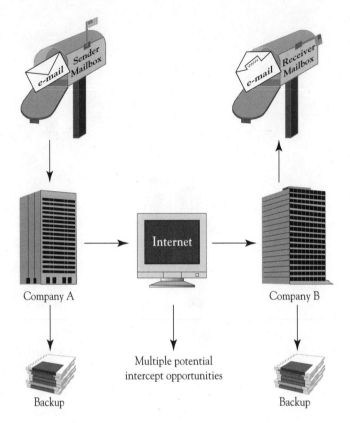

Figure 2.2 Example of corporate e-mail route over the Internet.

be intercepted by "packet sniffers"—software designed especially to intercept e-mails floating en route over the Internet.
Once the e-mail message finds the receiver's server, it passes
through company B's server, where it is backed up prior to
reaching the receiver's inbox. Because this process happens in
mere seconds or minutes, we do not see it or feel it. This may
help explain why our perceptions of e-mail at the user level
seem different from reality. E-mail's apparent simplicity and its

tremendous capability for widespread communication have created a false sense of security and privacy.

These diagrams give us a better appreciation of what can happen when sending and receiving e-mails. We can also see how little control we have over what happens to our e-mails in the short and long term. A casual, somewhat cocky message that's meant to be a joke could easily make its way to the news media if someone chooses to forward it, or into a lawyer's hands as part of a larger investigation. In addition, those with the knowledge to do so can use our e-mails against us. However, e-mail does contain an inborn element of democracy that protects us against such abuses. Two stories come to mind.

The first involves an individual who worked for a large software company and who was having an affair with the firm's president. She was dismissed and launched a wrongful termination suit, which she won after her lawyer discovered an e-mail in the president's inbox concerning the termination. Subsequently, the message proved to be a forgery that the terminated employee planted because she knew the president's password. She was countersued for evidence falsification and computer network intrusion. She lost.

The second story occurred at a global computer hardware firm where a disgruntled ex-employee accessed the corporate e-mail system via the Internet and repeatedly flooded the system with derogatory, nuisance messages. It was estimated that these messages reached as many as 35,000 employees at one time. After repeated attempts to block the employee's access, the company sought legal relief by requesting a permanent injunction. The court awarded the company the injunction based on the premise of trespass, which forbids the use of someone else's property without permission.

The fact remains that this newest communication channel is like a grizzly bear that can suddenly rouse from hibernation at any time. It's little wonder that companies are becoming more concerned over securing their electronic communications systems. The risks, as we shall see next, are getting too great to ignore.

HOW E-MAIL MESSAGES ARE USED AS LEGAL EVIDENCE

Question: What is e-mail?

a. A convenient way to send information to other parties

b. A way to retain an audit-trail or record an instruction or request

c. A lawyer's paradise

If you confidently chose items (a) and (b), and hesitated at choosing (c), you have just taken the first step toward understanding the context of all work-related e-mail messages. Indeed, though calling e-mail a lawyer's paradise may seem an exaggeration, a brief review of American legal articles on e-mail litigation reveals a number of similar interpretations:

- There may be gold in e-mail.
- Dial "E" for evidence.
- The smoking gun of the future.
- Litigation goldmine: E-mail messages can contain explosive discovery material.

The fundamental issue in using communication between parties as evidence in a legal proceeding is determining whether use of that channel carries with it a *reasonable expectation* of privacy by the individuals involved. For example, a conversation overheard in a crowded subway train would not be considered private, even if sensitive matters were being discussed. However, if the same conversation took place in an office behind closed doors and was overheard or recorded without the parties' knowledge, then the conversation would be considered inviolable because of the parties' reasonable expectations of privacy in attempting to shelter a sensitive conversation.

Unless there is prior notification (e.g., monitoring phone calls to ensure quality of customer service), recording landline telephone conversations without prior consent from the conversing parties is not legal. However, by the very nature of their technological dependence on common air waves, cellular telephones do not fall within the same legal envelope as landlines and may be intercepted at will. The addition of new technologies in communication channels has (1) increased individual access through time and place and (2) expanded legal access by reducing barriers to the information.

Because business documents are a common staple in the recorded expression of corporate or individual intent, there are many guidelines that govern lawyers' ability to examine them during legal procedures. While this chapter is in no way intended to replace professional legal advice, it is beneficial to be aware of the basic rules that govern the use of business documents as potential evidence in the United States.

The Federal Rules of Civil Procedure provide overall guidance on which business records can be examined or reviewed by independent or third-party lawyers to determine their relevance to a particular issue in dispute. This is the procedure known as *discovery*. In 1970, an amendment to the discovery rule extended the reach of information to include computer data or data compilations. During the 1990s, the definition of computer-generated information was extended to include e-mails. An e-mail that is part of a discovery does not automatically become admissible evidence. This area is governed by the Federal Rules of Evidence.

While these two guidelines are applicable to the federal court system, many states have adopted their own codes for what constitutes evidence within their respective courtrooms. State codes may vary significantly from federal codes, so it may be prudent to verify and/or establish what is applicable within the state(s) where you are conducting business. Embedded within the rules of evidence are standards for *relevance, authenticity, and best evidence*. This code can be applied to e-mail as follows:

- Is the information that is contained in an e-mail related to the central issue in question? Does it provide reinforcement of key facts or actions?
- Can the e-mail message be specifically linked to an individual or situation and can you prove that it has not been tampered with or subsequently altered?

Under the best evidence rule, if the message can be reproduced directly from its original source—in this case, the computer's data storage—then a printed version can stand in place of an original document.

Within the rules of evidence there is a legal counterbalance that relates to the hearsay challenge, which purports that the content of some e-mail messages may be considered rumor, gossip, or nonbusiness related, and, therefore, should not be entered into evidence. However, if someone is lying or making the facts appear less than truthful, hearsay evidence may be permitted by the courts to support this notion.

The federal rules of evidence lay out a number of requirements for an e-mail message to be entered into evidence. These requirements include establishing that the message was created during business hours using the company's computer system, was expected as a regular practice to fulfill a business need, was made by an individual with firsthand knowledge of the situation, and within a period of time that establishes his or her current role in the situation. Finally, an individual with custodial responsibility for the e-mail system must attest to the trustworthiness of the record-keeping practices of the system itself. If an e-mail message can meet these burdens, then it can be used as evidence. Many workplace e-mails easily meet these standards.

What is it about e-mail that has captured lawyers' imaginations? What properties exist with e-mail that creates greater degrees of certainty for their use by the legal profession? A footnote taken from an article about using e-mail under the Texas rules of evidence describes it best, as follows:

> Electronic documents thought to be lost or destroyed can be recovered. Valuable information such as the time, date and author of a document may be embedded in the electronic version of the document. Comparisons of computer backups to existing documents can be used to show that a critical document was altered or destroyed and when such events occurred. And, in the case of electronic mail, casual

and candid correspondence can be frozen in time like an insect in amber.*

A sobering thought indeed.

UNDER WHAT CIRCUMSTANCES DO E-MAILS BECOME SMOKING GUNS?

We have now seen how easily e-mails can enter the legal system, and how, as a communication channel, electronic mail is far from private. It may be inexpensive and easy to use, but there are also increased opportunities for instances of poor judgment when we continue to underestimate the far-reaching power of electronic communication.

There are a variety of characteristics that differentiate electronic and written communication. The first as mentioned earlier is control—senders relinquish control once they press the send button. The second is representation—sending an e-mail from work is comparable to sending a letter using corporate stationery. Receivers of electronic mail may place more weight on messages because they appear to represent a corporate expression. The last characteristic that makes electronic mail unique is its lack of confidentiality. For example, it is easy to send and intercept proprietary or copyrighted information that represents the intellectual capital developed within a firm. This information can be sent either deliberately or unknowingly. With

---

*Joan E. Feldman and Rodger I. Kohn, *The Essentials of Computer Discovery*, The Technology Answer Show Conference and Exhibition Glasser Legal Works 297, 299 (1998).

so much at stake, it's no wonder that an increasing number of companies are monitoring their electronic communications.

Even before the ubiquity of e-mail in the workplace, companies had concerns about productivity issues, employee harassment, defamation, and breaches in confidentiality. Safeguards in the form of procedures, processes, and codes of conduct were implemented to help minimize these concerns and provide adequate checks and balances into the system. Electronic mail systems provide a new platform that works against many previously established corporate safeguards.

Companies risk civil and/or criminal liability from both the intentional and unintentional misuse of their technologies. This is why many companies now use software to monitor their electronic communications. The challenge in monitoring e-mail transmissions is trying to identify specific e-mails that may pose risks of legal action. The basic tool for monitoring e-mails is a keyword match, similar to those used by search engines, to sift out and highlight only those e-mails that may be suspect. The problems arise from the context of certain words, which, depending on their use, may signal a contentious issue. An example is the word *breast*. If you are working on various client accounts for supermarkets or sportswear companies, then e-mails could be sent that contain words relating to chicken parts, a swimming stroke, or even a confession such as "making a clean breast of things." There is nothing wrong with this use, yet the word might be flagged as one that has potential problematic use. Clearly, it is important to use our best judgment in composing e-mails. It is critical for organizations to work to develop sophisticated monitoring procedures that allow for complex variations in use of language. A monitoring system that is too inclusive becomes very expensive since a person or persons must sift through the flagged electronic communications to determine which ones are problematic.

A more common problem that many organizations have is how to minimize e-mail messages that contain informal or sarcastic banter that can be taken out of context when read at face value. Our Wall Street example was a case in point on committing casual remarks and opinions to e-mail. Employees may engage in a type of gallows humor within their organizations that serves to provide comic relief in meetings and other verbal interactions. When these become documented, they take on a much different hue. For instance, in 2003, a New York judge ruled that e-mails relating to an employment-discrimination case against an investment banking firm be produced for discovery—at the firm's expense. At issue is the number of files the plaintiff's lawyers are allowed to review to support their case. Currently, the judgment is restricted to a few files. One lawyer in the case indicated that he hopes these files will be "littered with commentary," so they can review more of the firm's e-mails. Even before e-mail, lawyers saw internal comments on documents such as "this product is hot stuff or we are ripping our customers off," as a smoking gun. The challenge is to create awareness of these potential liabilities without staunching the flow of information or stifling personality or creativity.

Many companies are working hard to protect corporate performance and exposure to liability while protecting their employees' legitimate concerns over privacy. Yet, since 1997, surveys from the American Management Association (AMA) have shown that an increasing number of companies—in the 2002 survey this figure is well over 50 percent—are reviewing and recording their employees' communications. This trend is expected to continue. The 2002 survey also indicated that 25 percent of firms dismissed employees for abusing use of the electronic mail system or the Internet while at work. You can almost predict where a trend is going by paying close attention to the products and services that have entered the marketplace to address electronic mail issues. Some commercial insurers, for example, are now offering e-insurance policies to minimize the impact that first-party loss and third-party claims may have on companies. An increasing number of software vendors are creating electronic-discovery tools to make it easier for lawyers to search e-mail records and documents by keyword, rather than manually.

So far, our discussion has focused the causes of electronic mail driven litigation and the impact of such litigation on both individuals and organizations. Let's now turn our discussion to what we can more proactively do within the workplace to prevent these legal surprises.

PREVENTATIVE MEASURES: A GUIDE FOR YOURSELF AND YOUR ORGANIZATION

Do Not Commit Anything to E-mail that You Would Not Want to Read on the Front Page of the *New York Times*. Electronic Mail Is Like a Postcard—Anyone Can Read It

We must accept greater individual responsibility with each e-mail message we write. It is impossible to control the ultimate and final destination of any message, but we can increase our awareness to ensure that we do not commit sensitive information to e-mail messages. The broad categories of sensitive information include human resource issues, competitive intelligence, intellectual capital, and/or trade secrets, insider knowledge regarding organizational changes, and financial dealings. Regardless of the industry you work in or the sophistication of the e-mail technology (encrypted, protected) that you use, you should carefully consider any correspondence that touches on these sensitive areas. Electronic mail correspondence that does involve these areas should be composed with the same professional regard as a letter being prepared to a client or shareholder. Carelessness, boasting, personal thoughts, gossip, and pet names have no place in corporate e-mails. This point is designed to drive home the fact that you should never consider your e-mails to be private information. There are laws in place that permit scrutiny of e-mail in many broad circumstances.

For instance, to expand the scope of the 1968 Wiretap Act, Congress passed the Electronic Communications Privacy Act in 1986. The Act aimed to balance "the privacy interests of telecommunication users, the business interests of service providers, and the legitimate needs of government investigators."* The AMA study we mentioned earlier bears repeating—over 50 percent of employers indicated that they monitor employees' e-mail and Internet usage. Yet there is nothing in this statute that compels employers to advise their employees of these activities, so it is best to assume that your employer can read or intercept any e-mail message that you write. This does not mean that employers and organizations actively read their employees' messages. No employer has time or resources for this task. Employers are primarily concerned about protecting their legitimate business

---

*The Electronic Frontier: The Challenge of Unlawful Conduct Involving the Use of the Internet. A Report of the President's Working Group on Unlawful Conduct on the Internet, March 2000. http://www.usdoj.gov /criminal/cybercrime/unlawful.htm.

interests while ensuring that their employees work in a safe and harassment-free environment.

Employers may also monitor e-mail messages in an attempt to determine which messages should be stored and which should be expunged. In this way, they try to reduce their costs and their vulnerability to legal investigations.

Remember That There Is No Such Thing as Deleted Electronic Mail

You should view e-mails as permanent records. The misconception that many of us have about being able to delete or destroy an electronic message is a dangerous one. The data is stored indefinitely and more and better technologies are being developed to recapture it. Some companies employ expunge policies that periodically eradicate old electronic records from the company server. However, e-mail records may still reside on the recipients' systems and can be recovered for legal use. The best course of action is to regard e-mail as permanent and use it only for professional, legitimate, and publicly known information.

Protect Your E-mail Account

Don't think that e-mail systems are secure and inviolate in the workplace. Protect access to your e-mail account through passwords and/or locking your office door when you are not in. Don't unnecessarily expose yourself to having someone else use your e-mail account to send potentially illegal or damaging information on your behalf. It may be extremely difficult to prove that you did not send the message.

SOLUTIONS FOR THE ORGANIZATION

One obvious solution is to create policies for workplace e-mails that will guide employees' actions. My own research has shown that over 70 percent of people feel strongly that companies should take the lead role in assisting employees to be more productive e-mail users. A growing number of companies are creating policies, which differ in their level of comprehensiveness and implementation. This section highlights three specific areas where companies can begin this process.

Banners

Many organizational guidelines are tied into the corporate code of conduct and remind people of their professional responsibilities regarding their use of offensive materials and language. Some organizations use network banners—standard messages that are attached to every electronic message. Network banners notify e-mail users of their legal rights. The U.S. Department of Justice files on cybercrime search and seizure offer several examples of network banner language that can help protect organizations. The requirements for banners can be broad, covering every area of computer access (used especially for highly classified materials), or narrow, covering specific items such as monitoring transmissions. An example they provide covering broader network access is:

> You are about to access a United States government computer network that is intended for authorized users only. You should have no expectation of privacy in your use of

this network. Use of this network constitutes consent to monitoring, retrieval, and disclosure of any information stored within the network for any purpose including criminal prosecution.

The following are two banner examples that cover network monitoring situations:

> This computer network belongs to XYZ Corp. and may only be used by its employees for work-related purposes. XYZ Corp. reserves the right to monitor use of this network to ensure network security and to respond to specific allegations of employee misuse. Use of this network shall constitute consent to monitoring for such purposes. In addition, XYZ Corp. reserves the right to consent to do a valid law enforcement request to search the network for evidence of crime within the network.

> It is the policy of ABC firm to monitor the Internet access and e-mails of its employees to ensure compliance with our firm's policies. Accordingly, your use of both the Internet and e-mail systems may be monitored. The firm reserves the right to disclose the fruits of any monitoring to law enforcement if it deems such disclosure to be appropriate.

Banners can provide general admonitions on the context of e-mails, explaining why certain information should not be transmitted, that is, copyright, proprietary, trade secrets, and the like. While banners can provide some level of notification and protection, very few e-mail policies describe in depth the types of information that should go into electronic messages to begin with or what roles a department manager or executive play in reinforcing these policies.

Formulating E-mail Guidelines

Although most organizations do not have guidelines for other communication channels, we've seen that electronic mail is in a category all its own. Its misuse in the workplace can contribute to inefficiency and inappropriate messaging. When so many of us are trying to grapple with the best way to use e-mail within different work environments, establishing general guidelines becomes a worthwhile investment of corporate time and energy. As we have seen in the first segment of this chapter, companies have nothing to lose.

An organization's e-mail policy should incorporate the following:

Purpose: Briefly outline the rationale for the e-mail policy. Describe protection from potential liability and better use of the system.

Scope: To whom does the policy apply?

Which systems does it cover?

Is there one global policy or will there be regional policies?

Ownership: Statements that reinforce the fact that the electronic mail system is a corporate resource and that all e-mail traffic is the property of the organization.

Liability: Indicate that e-mail is subject to disclosure during litigation proceedings.

Types of liability include: defamation, harassment, copyright penalties, infringement of tangible property rights, infringement of intellectual property rights, disclosure of trade secrets, criminal penalties.

Include a cautionary note that information that would not normally be committed to writing should not be transmitted by e-mail.

Indicate that all users are personally accountable for the messages that they originate and forward using company electronic mail systems.

System monitoring:	Disclose the nature and use of surveillance software that protects individual employees and company information.
Policies on expunging:	Briefly explain how this works for deleted e-mail and the company's retention policy.
Appropriate use:	The system should not be used in ways that are disruptive and offensive to others and inconsistent with the organization's professional image.

Information of a confidential, sensitive, or otherwise proprietary nature is not to be disclosed.

Use for personal purposes permitted within reasonable boundaries. |
| *Corporate Intranet:* | Describe its purpose, its location, list of all employee bulletin boards, what to post, and procedures. |
| *E-mail protocols:* | Define the scope of acceptable e-mail traffic—that is, in the performance of job-related functions.

Outline the types of information that should be posted on the Intranet.

Explain how distribution lists are used.

Describe appropriate use of forwarding, reply-to-all, and corresponding-copy functions. |

Emphasize brevity and clarity of messages.

Describe acceptable message tone and professional formatting—what lengths are optimal.

Identify restrictions with use and/or size of file attachments, especially for remote e-mail users.

Suggest ways users can archive and remove e-mail from boxes and folders.

Virus protection: Inform users about the nature of the system's operation.

Caution users about opening unknown attachments or floppy discs.

Explain procedures to follow if a virus message appears.

Contact information: Indicate where employees can seek further information and/or provide feedback and inputs.

TIPS FOR DEVELOPING GUIDELINES

Developing electronic mail guidelines is a challenging task that is worth a company's effort. The key is to be brief and concise while using plain language. Because of the potential legal liabilities involved in using corporate e-mail, it is important to expose these issues without making the policy read like a legal document. Words and tone play an important role in how employees will respond to these guidelines.

Establishing e-mail guidelines can be a critical first step in taming the corporate e-mail system and encouraging more productive behavior. But developing guidelines is not enough. Managers need to be involved in their execution by making presentations and holding discussions within their departments. A clear understanding of the policy's overall goals and its benefits for all employees will foster better long-term management of organizational communication. Here are some tips for doing just that:

1. Designate leadership of e-mail policy development to an individual outside of Information Technology (IT) or Management Information Systems (MIS). While IT professionals may be involved in providing system-related information (i.e., expunge policies), this type of initiative should be seen clearly as a management responsibility.

2. Involve a cross-section of individuals from all corporate ranks to develop an accurate picture on the issues that exist with e-mail use. This will set the right direction and tone for a comprehensive e-mail policy that everyone will support.

3. Spend the time seeking an alignment of views and perspectives within the organization regarding e-mail problems and solutions. An e-mail policy should serve the needs of all employees if it is to create a more productive communication system. Include individuals who don't believe there is an e-mail problem in their particular work area—their perspective could be invaluable in the process.

4. An electronic mail policy or guidelines should serve to motivate and energize individual employees and corporate departments rather than acting as a control or temporary problem-solving mechanism. Leaders should consistently articulate an e-mail policy's vision (time

and money saved) and benefits to employees (time saved, more efficiency, less stress) throughout the organization.

5. Take advantage of an e-mail policy by using it to communicate to broad groups within the organization. Create a communication plan for effectively distributing the electronic mail policy within the organization. Managers should design this plan to reach as many internal audiences as possible.

DEVELOPING E-MAIL RETENTION POLICIES

There are three steps for organizations to consider when creating an e-mail retention policy—identifying the problems, searching for potential solutions, and crafting the plans.

There are three areas where e-mail retention poses issues for organizations:

1. *Discovery*. Electronic mail produces near permanent records of everything placed on the system. Given the mix of readily available electronically based information coupled with the legal ease of requesting it, many companies are dangerously close to becoming unwitting and unwilling drinkers of this toxic brew.

2. *Disruption*. The second problem occurs when a company receives a subpoena requesting all electronic records that transpired between specific dates. This is not much of a problem if the time span is short (a week) and the organization does not rely heavily on e-mail

communication. But what if lawyers request all the various departmental records of a Fortune 500 company for a three-month period? If 2,000 employees who send an average of 48 e-mails a day are involved, in three months over 8.6 million e-mail records will have been produced. This volume may sound incredible; so let's assume that there are 50 employees in the same scenario. This would equate to 216,000 e-mail records that require review and sorting, which is still not a task that can be completed overnight.

If your organization has ever been involved in a lawsuit, whether lodged by a single employee, by another company, or by a regulator, then you know that the efforts to respond involve many parties and are a huge drain on corporate resources. Add to that the hassle of sorting through hundreds or thousands of e-mail records and it becomes a nightmare.

3. *Cost*. The cost of manually reviewing and sorting through e-mail records is substantial, if not prohibitive. Depending on the time frame of the request and the number of records involved, some cases have cost companies millions of dollars. From a legal perspective, companies do not have a choice in the matter—noncompliance has its own set of penalties that can be equally prohibitive. If there was ever a case for organizations to exercise some restraint when it comes to using their e-mail systems, this is it.

Now that we understand the problems, the next step is to look at potential solutions.

E-mail retention issues are not the sole domain of the IT professional. It is a fallacy to think that the in-house IT staff can resolve all things pertaining to technology. This thinking is similar to presuming that all doctors, be they general practitioners, specialists, or surgeons, are equally able to diagnose any medical ailment. The complexities of medical science are such that doctors specialize within a specific branch of medicine, and we need to view the IT professional in a similar fashion. When assessing an organizations' e-mail retention, it's important to work with information management professionals who have specific skills, knowledge, and experience in these matters.

To prepare for meetings with records professionals, the senior management team should be able to discuss the following issues.

Strategy

At what level or levels within the organization will we apply responsibility for e-mail retention, archiving, organizing, and permanent deletion? Will we do this at the end-user level, by division, by strategic business unit, or companywide? Our choices will affect costs and long-term viability. For instance, driving this process at the end-user level, while initially cost effective, may result in additional burdens being placed on IT personnel who will need to assist end-users in retrieving archived documents and old messages. Applying responsibility at a higher level may cost more initially, but it may be more efficient and productive in the long run. Much will depend on the organization's configuration and its industry base.

Policy

What are the regulatory or statute requirements that govern retention of business-critical information? Records pertaining to
employment issues such as tax and payroll may fall under one set
of guidelines while other records fall under different guidelines.
Records pertaining to client information, especially in regulated
industries such as financial services, will have very specific retention requirements for differing levels of information. Currently, all companies regulated by the U.S. Securities and
Exchange Act must keep communications relating to their
client dealings for three years. This definition is broad and,
therefore, firms must take extra steps to determine what types of
e-mail information fall within this definition prior to determining how the information will be stored. For decades, many companies have worked within retention guidelines designed for
paper documents. This would be a good place to start when trying to assess the scope required for electronic communication.

Another consideration is to examine any national standards
or protocols that are emerging or are in existence on electronic
records management issues. In 1999, the United Kingdom and
France created national standards to govern electronic document and record management in light of legal admissibility requirements. Currently, these countries are regarded as leaders in
this area and we would benefit from emulating their benchmark
or best practice considerations.

Both countries' standards comply with the new international standard ISO 15489 created in 2002, which pertains to
records management, regardless of media type, where an organization or business is obligated to maintain these records for

potential future examination. This standard was created to ensure that appropriate protection is given to all records, and that evidence and information they contain can be retrieved more efficiently and effectively. "This standard identifies the key issues involved in retaining information and making it available in a useable and reliable way, as well as how it may be selectively and securely disposed of at the appropriate time."* It also works within other well-known ISO standards and would definitely be worth investigating as part of an organization's records management considerations.

Identification

How do we identify electronic information as business-critical and worthy of retention? One technology industry analyst has estimated that 60 percent of the information stored in a company's electronic files is considered business-critical. Even if this figure is accurate, it is a challenge to create a process or processes that make identification of relevant e-mails efficient and accurate throughout a large organization. Does it start at end-user levels? Should all electronic mail message subject lines contain an identifier? Should each e-mail be specifically tagged with a client or product code prior to sending to trace project or file accountability? We can see that establishing e-mail retention protocols is a complicated affair that impacts corporate processes and needs to be carefully considered for its long-term viability.

---

*New ISO standard for managing business records, *International Organization for Standardization*, Ref: 814, February 5, 2002. Available from http://www.iso.ch/iso/en/commcentre/pressreleases/2002/Ref814.html.

Developing solutions for managing electronic records is not an easy task. It requires corporate time, resources, and dedication, but much of this will be a one-time effort that will result in both short- and long-term benefits. If information is power, then could the methods a company uses to organize its electronic information become a competitive advantage?

The final step in our e-mail retention journey is crafting a policy that will breathe life into your corporate plans.

Policies that touch the surface of our corporate consciousness will always remain on the periphery while we toil with more immediate and measurable concerns. Policies that are reinforced and become integrated within the corporate culture have a much better chance of being adopted. For instance, if employees were periodically reminded that their e-mail messages could become part of a legal investigation, this could go a long way toward advancing responsible electronic mail behavior in the workplace. Three steps that help us to get positive employee input and support are as follows:

1. *Representative involvement in policy development.* A representative group needs to be responsible for creating and debating any policy that serves to protect both the company and its employees from litigation, harassment, and embarrassment. The policy also needs to be framed within the fabric of the corporate culture. An electronic communication policy is part of an evolution that embraces the new realities of technology in the workplace—not a revolution designed to overthrow all current practices.

    A cross-functional team of individuals from human resources, information technology management, corporate communications, and the legal department should be responsible for drafting the policy. This team should include senior executives who have corporate accountability and key managers who have a strong sense of employee and customer issues.

Once the first draft is prepared, it should be distributed to representatives from all corporate departments for their feedback. All concerns should be noted, addressed, and incorporated as part of the final policy document. There is no point in asking for input if it won't be used—this is the quickest way to ensure that the policy will receive the cold-shoulder from employees.

Finally, a communication plan should be drafted in such a way to ensure that all company employees are made aware of the policy and have an opportunity to discuss its meaning with their immediate superiors.

2. *Enlisting management's long-term support.* All individuals with supervisory responsibilities not only need to embrace the policy but need to endorse and support it whenever practical. They need to become more attuned to their departments' norms and behaviors regarding written and e-mail communication and provide guidance at appropriate moments. This does not mean that all managers and executives should read and investigate all electronic communications. It simply means adopting a greater awareness of the style, tone, and content of e-mails that originate within their departments.

3. *Reinforcement at end-user levels.* Whether this takes the form of employee training or an information push, specific guidelines need to be readily available that assist

end-user behavior and task modification. The information needs to go beyond well-worn homilies such as, "write what you mean and mean what you write," or "careful what you write, someone's watching." These serve very little purpose and can discredit a policy that's designed to protect mutual corporate interests.

To be valuable for employees, guidelines should be specific and include the following:

1. The risks of committing information to e-mail
2. The consequences that can occur
3. Examples of undesirable e-mail communication
4. A process for planning which communication channels to use for information
5. Examples of proper e-mail communication
6. Informing employees about where they can go to seek further advice and guidance for specific situations

This chapter outlined many issues that we may not have previously considered when using electronic mail. At the beginning of the chapter, we asked an innocent question "Why would anyone want to read my e-mail?" After reading this chapter, no doubt you have many more answers than you thought you might have had. You should also have new questions on how to become a more proficient user of your own electronic mail. The good news is that help is on its way. The remaining chapters in this book are devoted to helping you find the answers you need to succeed in the world of e-mail. Our next chapter, "Using E-mail Judiciously," takes a detailed look at choosing e-mail as an appropriate communication channel.

CHAPTER 3

Using E-mail Judiciously

Every day we make choices about how we share information. We dash off a note of thanks to a friend, meet colleagues for lunch, or post a message on an electronic
bulletin board. The communication choices we make shape
how the recipient responds to our message.

Is a written message better than a verbal one? It depends
on the message itself. If you were a human resources manager
advising several job candidates that they won't be hired, a
written explanation is probably the most considerate choice,
because it allows the receiver an opportunity to read the news
in private and reflect on this decision without having to deal
with others. In contrast, if a man writes a note to a woman to
let her know that he cares for her, she may disregard the message and wonder why he didn't tell her in person. Expressions
of sentiment require the richness of communication, both

verbal and nonverbal, which we can only convey in a face-to-face setting. In this case, choosing the wrong method for transmitting the message may do some damage. Imagine your reaction to the following scenarios:

- You receive a letter through the interoffice electronic mail system that you have been promoted.

  Reaction: While the message brings good news, you are apprehensive. Almost immediately after you get the news, you begin to wonder why your superior (with whom you thought you had a good rapport) didn't tell you himself? After all, most of us expect good news to be shared personally. Receiving a memo (especially when the boss is in the office and available), again casts doubt on whether this is really a promotion or is something wrong? Worse, this type of e-mail can raise self-doubt about your career and your security. The best approach here is to share good news of a personal nature using the matching medium—in this case a face-to-face meeting. If the news cannot wait, but the boss is away from the office on business, a telephone call conveying the news (and a promise of a celebratory drink) will give the equivalent message.

- You are a marketing manager. For the past year you have prepared a written report for your vice president and delivered it on time, every Monday without fail to her office. One Monday, the vice president walks into your office, sits down, and announces that, in the spirit of better communication, she wants to receive the report verbally, for the next couple of weeks.

Reaction: In this scenario, the vice president's desire to suddenly have more face-to-face communication with you through a routine work issue raises your concerns. You might interpret the announced change in plans as thoughtless, even rude. Communicating a written report verbally seems inefficient. Moreover, there is a channel mismatch between the media (face-to-face) and the information being delivered. You may well be wondering what the communication's real intention is. Are you coming under more scrutiny because you have done something wrong or is the vice president getting ready to fire you? The better approach here, if a more personal interaction were desired, would be for the vice president to ask you out for lunch, leaving routine matters as is.

- For the third time in a month, your supervisor cannot keep his appointment for the face-to-face weekly meeting and asks if the meeting can take place over the telephone.

  Reaction: In this scenario, the communication channel seems to shift from a higher to a lesser degree. While your supervisor's inability to meet face-to-face may be temporary, consecutive cancellations may be sending you the message that he is distancing himself from you, his subordinate. Even if your supervisor is truly overwhelmed with mission-critical projects, it is still important to establish that this seeming disconnect is temporary. The problem here is that this seems to be a form of communication starvation—almost the reverse of the first scenario with the same result. Unfortunately, these behaviors occur quite often in the workplace, especially if superiors know their employees may be potential candidates for termination. The best remedy here is for the supervisor either to share more information on the situation or to change the meeting day.

- Your colleague in the next office sends you an e-mail asking if you are free for lunch.

  Reaction: This scenario is becoming an office classic— "why doesn't she get up from her desk and ask me?" Again, this is a clear-cut case where a personal sentiment is being expressed in an impersonal way, and for many people, the medium conveys a confused, if not baffling message. One might wonder, "Is my colleague losing her human touch? Should I be rethinking my working relationship with this person? Is this person just assuming in advance I'll say yes?" It is easy enough to see how these reactions can occur with such a blatant misuse of a communication medium.

As we can see in each of these examples, communication has occurred, but the choice of channel has altered. In the recipient's mind, the meaning of the message is unclear.

Now imagine two scenarios involving a CEO addressing the company's employees during a crisis within the organization:

1. In scenario 1, the CEO reads from a carefully prepared statement and then leaves the stage.
2. In scenario 2, the CEO acknowledges the audience, reads from a carefully prepared statement, and then takes a couple of questions from the audience.

The basic message (the prepared statement) and the channel used (face-to-face) are identical in both scenarios. Yet, the responses to each are quite different because scenario 2 included an acknowledgment and two questions from the audience.

In scenario 1, a company's intention to inform employees personally of a situation is overshadowed by the stronger message that it does not care about its employees (the CEO left the stage after delivering the message). This type of communication can easily lower employee morale, which can result in lower productivity.

In scenario 2, the message and audience response are closely linked. The employees leave the meeting feeling valued and important to the company's future success. This was the original intention of the message.

Let us review the choices available for communication. We can define communication as managing messages to create shared understanding or meaning. We create meaning in two ways—by content (words, symbols, numbers) and by context (medium or channel).

The content of a message consists of the words, symbols, or numbers that we use to construct information. Message context refers to how the speaker or writer conveys information to the recipient. A message context is also called a *communication medium* or *communication channel*. Identified in Table 3.1, the channels of communication are face-to-face, telephone, e-mail, and written.

Of these four communication channels, face-to-face communication generally conveys the greatest content because of the many senses involved. This channel, therefore, has the highest information carrying capacity. Although Table 3.1 assumes communication in a common language, it is interesting

Table 3.1   Communication Channels: Basic Usage Definitions

Channel	Definition
Face-to-face	A two-way interaction using visual, verbal, and auditory skills
Telephone	A two-way interaction using only verbal and auditory skills
E-mail	A one-way transmission of specific content requiring recipient's visual skills to decipher (may transition to written if the e-mail is printed)
Written	A one-way transmission of complex, detailed, and/or lengthy content requiring recipient's visual skills to decipher information

to note that many of us who travel have found that face-to-face communication, even when a common language does not exist, can be quite effective because nonverbal communication has the power to convey meaning and intent. This principle does not apply to the other three forms of communication, however.

A business environment uses all four communication channels. The mix of these channels, along with the channel's suitability to the message constitutes a critical but often overlooked aspect of communication strategy within organizations.

Because organizations depend on communication to achieve their goals, it is crucial for them not only to select the right channels but also to design communication to ensure smooth, seamless feedback. Feedback is not simply an equivalent response in kind—it is measured by the receiver's response to the incoming message. Therefore, an electronic message that is ambiguous will likely elicit a response that either does not match the inquiry or requests greater clarity. Fast and accurate comprehension of the sender's intentions should be the goal of all communication, regardless of the channel used.

In 1987, American communication researchers conducted a study that revealed how and why managers chose particular channels for communication in the workplace.* The study polled 65 managers across medium and large U.S.-based organizations, and gathered specific information about managers' reasons for selecting any of the four communication channels—face-to-face, telephone, electronic mail, and written (the researchers did not distinguish between personal and wide-audience writings). Although e-mail was not as commonly used then, it was considered a recognized channel for business communication and included in the study.

The study found that managers tend to favor face-to-face communication when the development of ideas and team understanding are most important. They also use it as a way to reaffirm, establish, or assert authority and position power within work groups. Workplace tasks that for the most part are considered complex and nonroutine would fit into this category as would more routine tasks that involve high degrees of personal interaction. Developing relationships, negotiating, generating ideas, solving problems, resolving conflicts, discussing workplace performance, and making sales calls are instances in which face-to-face communication is critical.

Managers use the telephone for specific, urgent situations; for content-related issues; and for fine-tuning plans. They also use it to reinforce and extend relationships.

---

* Linda K. Trevino, Robert H. Lengel, and Richard L. Daft, *Communication Research*, 14 (October 5, 1987), pp. 553–574.

Managers use written communication to support content development and to supplement information that other channels convey. Written communication also confers authority on its creators. Examples of this are external consultants' reports, the findings of an internal task force, or a letter to all employees signed by the CEO.

Managers use electronic mail to handle lower priority information with little content and/or detail. Since the time of this study, there has been a huge shift in the use of electronic mail. Yet, this study was conducted at a time when we were well into the Information Age. We may infer that increased e-mail use has been drawn from the other three channels, with mixed results. Much of the tension we experience with e-mail stems from its overuse as a communication channel for delivering messages of varying complexity and meaning. Viewing the results of this study helps us put into better perspective the intended uses of various communication channels.

What Marshall McLuhan meant when he said, "The medium is the message" is that the medium (or channel) we use to record and transmit information has more impact on the information we are communicating than the information itself. Like Aristotle (whose principles we discuss in Chapter 5), McLuhan created his own brand of communication principles, which focused on how technology was changing communication patterns and influencing society. As we saw in Chapter 1, his theory of *technological determinism* was based on the premise that technological inventions within society give birth to cultural change. McLuhan asserted that throughout human history, changes in the modes of communication were largely responsible for molding our existence, and that each new mass communication tool created sweeping social changes.

Let's put his theory to the test. Consider the following dialog:

"Can you get that Lawson file for me?"
"It is in your office cabinet."
"Where?"
"Look under the section labeled marketing research."
"Found it. Thanks."

This conversation is a typical office exchange between a manager and an assistant, right? Wrong. It is actually five separate e-mail messages between two parties who sit a few feet apart from one another.

Why do messages like these occur so often in the workplace? Why doesn't the manager stop by the employee's office or call? Why bother sending an e-mail chain like this?

The operative word in this scenario is "bother." Why do people bother to send e-mail when their message would be better communicated using a more efficient method? The manager in this conversation is obviously not bothered in the least about initiating this series of electronic mail communications.

Part of the problem we face in dealing with technology is managing the assumption that it is a *zero-sum* game. In other words, if we do not wholly embrace e-mail technology, we are not taking full advantage of its capabilities. However, this idea is similar to believing that computers and e-mail would eradicate paper. This same notion has resurfaced with regard to e-mail, but it does not really make sense. In fact, electronic mail can actually be less efficient as this example shows. It would have been much easier and more time-efficient for the manager to make the inquiry in person. The matter of the missing file could have been settled quickly. The back-and-forth e-mail messages not only took time for these individuals to compose and read, but the messages also interrupted their work—not once but three times. Multiply this example by the countless thousands of similar instances each day and you have a great deal of wasted time just because people chose to use e-mail over a more interpersonal channel of communication.

There is a broader human context when choosing to use e-mail, especially when an interactive channel would be more appropriate. When you know from both the message's content and the sender's proximity that calling or stopping by your office would have been more suitable, you, like most people in similar circumstances, may feel disconcerted. Worse yet, you may feel angry, hurt, or ignored. Dr. Edward Hallowell, a psychiatrist and lecturer at Harvard Medical School, who studied communication dysfunction in the workplace, coined the phrase "toxic worry" to describe the subtle sense of disconnection we feel when e-mail replaces communication that requires valuable human contact. Toxic worry is one of the reasons why so many of us feel a little more frustrated with e-mail each day and are looking for ways to cope. We are looking for solutions.

SOLUTIONS TO COMMUNICATION CHANNEL SELECTION

The first step toward solving potential communication confusion is to recognize when electronic mail is an appropriate channel and when other, more interactive communication channels are preferable. The following guidelines can help us make these decisions:

Communication Channel	Content Drivers
E-mail:	Formal communication for a specific purpose
	A distinct audience
	Fact-based request where nonverbal cues are not required
	Indirect, two-way transaction (i.e., send request, then receive response)
Telephone:	Less formal communication for one or two specific reasons
	An audience of one (conference calls excluded)
	Candid responses, discussion of common ideas, ability to establish conversational rapport
	Direct, interactive transmission that permits instant decision making
Face to face:	Choice of formalities, depending on subject and audience
	Permits high-content discussions, exploration of ideas, ability to deal with complex problems
	The only choice for sensitive, personal, or negative communication
	Direct, interactive, immediate feedback

One area that clearly distinguishes e-mail from both the telephone and personal contact is the static nature of the information exchange. With e-mail, there is a very specific cycle of transmission. I call this an *indirect transactional pattern,* as seen in Figure 3.1.

This sequence completes the e-mail communication cycle and the transaction itself. If the information that we request or desire cannot be readily delivered within the bounds of this model, we need a more interactive channel to enhance efficiency.

Electronic mail cannot replace the richness and efficiency of a conversation. There are minor exceptions to this, including one of e-mail's greatest benefits—the ability to communicate over multiple time zones. But even in this environment, international communication is highly punctuated and supplemented with both structured telephone calls and on-site visits.

Here are some tips to keep in mind when you're deciding whether or not to use electronic mail:

- Let the message content drive the medium you use to communicate. Don't telephone and e-mail looking for information or response for the same item—use either one or the other. It is perfectly acceptable to use the telephone to discuss the content of information-dense e-mails or to notify sending or receipt. These practices make use of

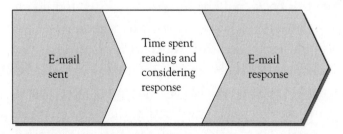

Figure 3.1 Communication sequence for e-mail.

multiple channels for workflow efficiency—phoning and e-mailing for an identical request do not.

- To encourage more human interaction, answer more complex e-mails by telephone or in person.

- If an e-mail message seems too difficult to type, then this may be a clear signal to you to select a more personal form of communication—either the telephone or in person.

- If you receive a message from someone who didn't understand your original request, or if you don't understand a message that someone has sent you, then pick up the telephone to provide or clarify the requested information.

Solutions for Managers: Reaching a Consensus on E-mail Use

If you're a manager, encourage a dialog within employee groups on how to use the e-mail communication channel and for what purpose(s). You can initiate this discussion by relating a personal story, for example, a particular e-mail moment that seemed wasteful or inappropriate. This would lead smoothly into a general discussion on the topic—people will not be shy in this area. Reading this book could be suggested as a step toward creating better understanding and more workable solutions.

In your discussions within departments or divisions, create guidelines on which types of information should be communicated via e-mail. Make sure employees agree that conveying these types of information through electronic mail will best serve their current needs for efficient communication and information exchanges. Again, this initiative could find its genesis in relating a personal story that you can use as a discussion topic with some of your colleagues in other departments. Such an informal chat would be a great forum to exchange topical information and share ideas.

Don't be afraid to reinforce e-mail guidelines in specific situations, and on a case-by-case basis. Emphasizing guidelines usually reaps great all-round benefits in improving department communications. Even after there's agreement on many procedural changes, there will always be situations where individual judgments and interpretations vary. Gentle reinforcement contributes so much more to understanding than do clear-cut, restrictive mandates.

ASSUMPTIONS ABOUT MESSAGE CONTEXT AND RECIPIENT'S RESPONSE TIME

"Ken, I want to chat with you about that new initiative your team is working on," his boss said during a chance meeting in the office corridor. "There are some issues that we need explore further before we can proceed with the project."

"I'm not sure what you mean. We have already proceeded with supplier commitments and implementation planning," replied Ken. "Besides, I sent you an e-mail that outlined our plans. I did not get a response, so I presumed that we had your blessing to proceed."

This scenario is typical of how we increasingly use electronic mail to inform other parties while assuming that they understand our context. We also assume that just because we have sent people an e-mail message, they have had all the time they need to read the message and make decisions based on the information we have communicated.

First, we tend to assume that the act of sending an e-mail absolves us of all responsibility for ensuring that the recipient is fully versed about a message's context and is in agreement with it. In these circumstances, we make assumptions about the recipient's time, electronic mail habits, and response capabilities.

Some e-mail messages can confuse the receiver who wastes time trying to decipher not only message content but also the reason for the approach. For example, executives who receive mysterious (cc) messages from their direct reports or managers who are one or two levels below their direct reports lament that these messages create inappropriate expectations. The individuals who send these messages seem to be trying, whether they are aware of it or not, to circumvent the chain of command.

Second, the time at which we decide to send supporting or follow-up materials for an upcoming presentation, meeting, or project can become problematic. Although e-mail permits quick and easy sending of documentation, materials or information may be sent too late in the workday to be retrieved and printed, let alone reviewed.

The seemingly instantaneous nature of the e-mail channel encourages the compression of timelines and deadlines for editing and approvals. Before e-mail attachments existed, people would manually forward stacks of paper for review and consideration. One person I interviewed talked about receiving a 50-page document by e-mail just 24 hours before the final deadline for her review and sign off. Prior to e-mail, she would have had at least 72 hours to review the same document.

The notion of compressed deadlines most likely occurs because we mistakenly believe that a new immediacy has emerged with the transfer of information by e-mail. Yes, there is immediacy, but it is with distribution and not with processing and review times. In some instances, this situation amounts to nothing more than someone being late with the deliverable and using e-mail as the "date-stamp" to establish completion of their part of the project. This becomes most obvious when several departments are working toward a common deadline and you are at the mercy of other people's workflows. In some instances, a date-stamp becomes a more important individual performance indicator than whether the actual item arrived during working hours. For many people, an item arriving at 11:00 P.M. on the due date, rather than 12 hours earlier, is considered late delivery.

A related concern we have about e-mail is its timeliness. Many of us express frustration at being informed too late about a changing situation by e-mail. The sender presumes that once the message is sent, the reader has read the message, understood it, and taken some kind of action. Recipients need time to read and acknowledge relevant information.

Solutions

What are the solutions to context and timing issues?

1. Don't presume that the act of sending an e-mail automatically confers agreement or acceptance by your reader. Request a response electronic mail or a meeting.

2. Remember that although you can send and receive e-mail over cyberspace instantaneously, your reader's review of your e-mail messages must fit in with their individual work routines. Ensure adequate time for your recipients to review large and complex documents or presentations, regardless of the channel you used to deliver these materials.

ASSUMPTIONS ABOUT E-MAIL RELEVANCE

We make many assumptions about e-mail's place within a business framework. What is relevant, what is not; when does an e-mail convey accountability and when does it not; should we use e-mail to document all business transactions?

I asked people to define what constitutes a relevant e-mail message. Here are the most popular answers:

- The message contains information I need to know that contributes to decision making.
- The message contains critical information about the organization and my department.
- The message contains specific answers to requested information.
- E-mail messages from my superiors are relevant.
- The message contains information that helps me perform my job more effectively.

From these answers, it's clear that we expect e-mails to be informative. We want our information to be proactive, anticipated, and clearly related to our specific responsibilities. Many of us complain that the information in some e-mail messages feels like it is being hurled at us rather than specifically serving our needs. One pet peeve that executives cited frequently is the amount of e-mail that is copied to them or sent to them couched in terms of "this is for your information only." This type of message seems like an indirect request for agreement or approval. Some executives have simply reacted to these messages by refusing to confer agreement on anything that is not discussed with them first or where they have given a clear mandate.

The e-mail channel's dominance in the workplace makes it easy for us to envision that an information blanket covers everyone in an organization. Unfortunately, much of the information we disseminate throughout the workplace tries to cover too much territory, rendering its specific value useless.

Another misuse of e-mail worth emphasizing is its overuse as a paper trail. A discussion is taking place, and suddenly someone requests that you summarize the discussion in an e-mail. I call this being enlisted to prepare someone else's notes. Why should they take notes, when you will agree to prepare the electronic version for them?

This is often an irrelevant and counterproductive use of electronic mail.

What Are Some Solutions to These Common Problems?

Certainly the key to managing these problems is vigilance and awareness of the channel's appropriate use. Do not automatically use e-mail as the default mode for business communication. Keep in mind that before e-mail existed, many relevant items, but not everything, were committed to paper memos.

Discussion and note taking remain some of the most valuable communication tools in the workplace.

Do not presume that copying someone on an e-mail will automatically gain you approval or authority to act. In an effort to manage their inboxes, some people color-code their "copy" e-mails to distinguish them from the messages that are sent directly to them. Personally addressed e-mails generally receive top priority. If the person to whom you are copying is receiving 70 or more e-mails a day, it may be days before he or she reads your message, if at all. If you want to confirm approval or awareness of a situation, tell the individual in person or use the telephone. If you want to commit yourself in writing, then send an e-mail message directly to that person.

Practice vigilance toward people who want to conduct everything by electronic mail. The workplace relies on a variety of communication channels to conduct business and the e-mail channel should be just one part of this mix. Use e-mail when it is efficient, productive, and appropriate, for both the message and the receiver. At times, electronic mail senders forget these principles in favor of doing what is convenient for them.

PROBLEMS RELATED TO CORPORATE CULTURE

Here are some of the problems that I have found in my work with corporations:

- In a discussion with a group of senior managers on e-mail practices within their company, conversation centered on their corporation's expectations about employees' being computer accessible on a 24/7 basis. There seemed to be much angst in the room on this issue. I then asked if this was a formal policy, and everyone went silent. So I changed tactics and asked how they came to believe that this was the case. Their response was that they received numerous e-mails from senior management over the weekends.

- A field superintendent is overwhelmed by e-mail because his employees keep letting him know every time they finish a task, no matter how large or small. Before e-mail was introduced to the unit, he heard only about problems that needed to be resolved. Now he has, in effect, a chat line to manage.

- A consultant sends a message to a partner in the firm. The message does not relate to a project that they are working on but rather is intended to create some visibility for himself for future assignments. Given the sophistication of their e-mail system, the consultant could discern when his partner actually opened and read the e-mail. Imagine his shock when the e-mail system's automated response advised him that the message was deleted without being opened.

These stories outline various misuses of the e-mail communication channel in the workplace. E-mail etiquette guidelines cannot help here because these situations fall into the broader context of corporate culture.

In the first story, employees are under the impression that the road to success is to check e-mail seven days a week.

Nothing is ever explicitly stated to this effect, but the strong, tacit understanding remains. People in this group believe this because they receive e-mail from senior executives outside standard working hours. Most employees attempt to model their supervisors, hence the impression that 24/7 is the expected work time.

The second story is another familiar scenario where e-mail is used to "keep in touch," despite nothing explicit ever being said to that effect. It appears that electronic mail is designed to keep everyone connected. Because it is cheap, easy to use, and available, electronic mail can promote constant updating, better contact, and ultimately relationship building.

The third story illustrates how the political use of e-mail can backfire. Some people would encourage using e-mail for "personal profiling." Many others feel that this practice is intrusive and a waste of corporate time. Some wish that software designers would come up with a way to create the "return to sender" e-mail that lets the sender know that her or his message was, by virtue of its content, unwanted and therefore unread.

Solutions

To alleviate some of these problems, a matching action by department managers and their organizations must be undertaken. In these situations, we are dealing with the direction of communication, either top-down or bottom-up.

Managers should refrain from sending e-mail outside standard business hours. This is especially true for senior executives, whose behaviors set a standard for their subordinates. If you must compose e-mail over the weekend, work in off-line mode and send e-mail messages the next available business day. If you are an executive, discourage your colleagues and senior staff from sending e-mails outside regular business hours as dictated by their time zone.

This suggestion also applies to subordinates. While the practice of sending e-mail messages all hours of the day and night may have impressed your superiors during e-mail's early days, it may now actually signal something else to superiors, who may wonder why you're working so late. Are you doing this to impress them or are you really not working efficiently during the normal workday?

Don't initiate progress reports by e-mail, unless your superior specifically invites you to do so. E-mail is not well suited to keeping a running dialog about daily activities. The intended audience—usually a superior—is not waiting at a computer for these messages. The "all's well at this end" type of message has a very short shelf life to be considered effective as communication. By the time most people read this kind of message, hours or even days may have passed and its impact is nil.

Don't use e-mail to raise your own profile in the organization. It is best to use the e-mail channel to exchange relevant information that helps the receiving parties perform their jobs. Don't use e-mail communication to enhance your corporate profile—let your actions and job performance speak for you instead. The substance of your message can put your reputation on the line. As a result, each disingenuous electronic mail becomes a liability, not an asset.

CLASSIC E-MAIL CHANNEL ABUSES

You're probably all too familiar with the following complaint:

> I hate e-mail ping-pong! Why doesn't someone just pick up
> the phone.

This quote gets to the heart of what I call the "asynchronous blues." Both written and e-mail communication are asynchronous in that the nature of the medium disrupts the exchange of ideas—there is no opportunity for immediate interaction. In contrast, verbal communications, whether they are face-to-face or by telephone, are synchronous—they occur within the same time frame. The asynchronous blues occurs when e-mail is used as a proxy for synchronous communication. It is channel confusion at its best and a frustrating time waster at its worst.

When we use e-mail as a convenient substitute for other forms of communication, many people silently despair at the absurdity of our choice. The following are five common abuses of the electronic mail channel:

1. Announcing last minute changes to meeting times/ places
2. Using e-mail for topics that obviously require personal contact or discussion
3. Using e-mail as the only channel with which people can communicate with you
4. Sending an e-mail message to a colleague who works in your immediate vicinity

5. Using the corporate e-mail system to vent anger about a workplace situation

Let's address each one of these abuses in more detail.

Announcing Last Minute Changes to Meeting Times/Places

Many of us express dismay at being advised late in the day that a change has occurred for a meeting taking place the next morning. We feel that there is a uniform expectation that we must constantly check and read all of our e-mail messages to keep abreast of new information. This smacks of too much connectivity, a condition that many of us are actively trying to avoid.

Using E-mail for Topics That Require Personal Contact or Discussion

Another key example of channel confusion is the e-mail message that should never have been sent in the first place. Have you ever wondered why you didn't get a response to your e-mail when you expected one? It may be because you have crossed over the asynchronous line. Either the topics in your message were too sensitive or controversial or you covered too many issues for the reader to assimilate. Some people even use e-mail to resolve differences of opinion or explain procedure. If there was ever a reason to pick up the telephone or even to meet colleagues in person, it is this one. In the workplace, misunderstandings and misinterpretations occur in the best of circumstances and e-mail simply is not the way to resolve them.

Using E-mail as the Only Channel through Which People Can Communicate with You

You love e-mail and therefore think that everyone else feels the same way. Many executives and managers are not quite sure when e-mail will eclipse our standard multichannel work world, but until it does, those people who choose to hide behind their computers may find themselves marginalized. Sending e-mails does not equate to being accessible, let alone accountable. Further, this type of evasive behavior creates barriers in the workplace that annoy and frustrate people who are seeking a more robust discussion on certain issues.

Sending an E-mail Message to a Colleague Who Works in Your Immediate Vicinity

Remember the chain of back and forth e-mail messages between the manager and employee that we used at the beginning of the chapter? It was clear that in that situation, it would have been more efficient for the manager to speak with the employee in person. For some of us, one of the most annoying situations occurs when a coworker or colleague within the same general office location sends us an e-mail message. The reaction is exacerbated the closer the sender sits to your desk or office. Many of these messages leave us puzzled as to why the person just didn't come by to talk to us. It is as if the e-mail system has erected some sort of impenetrable wall within the office. Always keep in mind that the medium we use to communicate speaks volumes and takes precedence over the message itself.

Research has shown that our needs for human interaction in the workplace are quite instinctive. Electronic communication serves a valuable purpose, but it does not replace nor supplant the other forms that create meaning and texture. In the eloquent words of another respondent, "technology may have come a long way, but humans haven't changed much in the past 2,000 years."

Using the Corporate E-mail System to Vent Anger about a Workplace Situation

My favorite illustration of this abuse occurred in Philadelphia in 1996 at a well-known consumer-goods company. An employee who was upset with his firm sent an e-mail message to a colleague referring to their mutual employer as "back-stabbing bastards." A week later, after intercepting the e-mail message, the company fired the employee for unprofessional conduct. The employee sought relief from the Philadelphia district court, which ruled in the company's favor. The judge indicated that employers had the right to monitor transmissions initiated over corporately owned computer equipment and to make judgments accordingly.

Many people are unaware that over 50 percent of U.S. companies monitor their employees' e-mail and Internet use. The level of monitoring varies from gathering records of time spent on Internet sites to highlighting certain key words in e-mail messages that match (much like the meta tags used for Web site search). At present, there are few precedents in North American law that require organizations to formally advise their employees that they are monitoring the employees' use of corporate computer equipment. Some companies tell their employees while others do not.

As we emphasized in Chapter 2, watch what you say in your e-mail messages because you don't know who may end up reading them. Also, always keep in mind that deleting your messages has no bearing on their continued existence in the company server. Whether an e-mail record is forever deleted will actually depend on a company's expunging policy and how often, if ever, the company eradicates old e-mail messages from its servers. Taking care about what you relate in your electronic mail messages is relevant to our next topic—using the e-mail channel to transmit content-sensitive information.

CHANNEL SECURITY AND CONTENT-SENSITIVE INFORMATION

As a rule, you should never send content-sensitive information under the assumption that e-mail systems are secure. Sensitive information (personnel, trade secrets, competitive intelligence, etc.) that is committed to electronic messages could later end up on a lawyer's desk. You should therefore be working under the assumption that all of your e-mail messages are retrievable at later dates (sometimes years).

My e-mail research reveals that we actually make conscious decisions not to commit certain information to an e-mail message. Indeed, there has been a shift in this attitude just within the past two years as people have developed a better understanding of e-mail use (and misuse). Table 3.2 illustrates the most popular answers my research participants gave in response to a

Table 3.2 Information Not to Be Sent by E-mail: Comparison of Two Studies

2001	2002
Private or privileged client materials	Human resource issues
Human resource issues (salary, job performance, career progression)	Messages that could be forwarded
Topics that require interactive dialog	Tone that could be misinterpreted
System secure—everything sent	Topics that require interactive dialog

question about the types of information that should not be sent through the e-mail channel.

These answers show an obvious shift in attitudes from one year to the next. Concerns surrounding privacy and privilege of client information seem to have given way to the convenience of using e-mail for transmitting information. This does not necessarily mean that people are unaware that electronic information can be intercepted. We can best interpret this attitude shift to mean that the parties in question understand the potential risks of interception and accept them for the sake of convenience. This notion is further supported by the change in attitude about the security of the e-mail system, which was the fourth ranked answer in 2001. We have much greater awareness about e-mail messages being used in high-profile legal cases. This awareness has created an attitude shift about e-mail's infallibility.

You already know how channel choice affects your message. It is interesting to note that the ubiquity of e-mail has not penetrated through the human resources barrier. For the overwhelming majority of respondents, human resource issues such as performance, salary, and career progression are sacred and, therefore, not appropriate topics for the e-mail channel. Unlike the change in attitudes regarding the transmittal of private or privileged client materials, our expectations about human resource related communications is clear—electronic mail is not an option.

At this point you may be wondering when you should use the e-mail channel? What are the benefits of using the e-mail channel?

BENEFITS OF THE E-MAIL CHANNEL

None of us wants to live without it, but we need to establish e-mail's proper place within the work environment. What do people really like about e-mail? Here are the most popular answers to this survey question:

- E-mail enables people to send and respond at their convenience.
- It encourages a quick response in real time.
- Electronic mail enables the sender to distribute the same message to many parties.
- E-mails provide an audit trail.
- It facilitates the easy transfer of data and information.

These responses tell us that productivity issues are indeed associated with electronic communication capabilities. Notice that interpersonal issues such as keeping in touch, building relationships, and sourcing new business are not cited among e-mail's most popular uses. Indeed, these answers seem to get right to the heart of how electronic mail is most effective in typical work situations.

First, our ability to control the time and place for e-mail communication underscores the asynchronous aspect of e-mail, especially for remote users or for users who are traveling on business. This level of connectivity is seen as a blessing, enabling the management of ongoing or routine situations from afar. Far from reducing business travel, e-mail can actually increase its frequency. Many users noted the capability to be easily connected to the office while on meaningful, client site visits. This created a powerful synchronicity between managing the ongoing (which did not require a physical presence) with establishing closer key client relationships (which did require human contact).

Second, we should not confuse the notion of receiving a quick response in real time with instant messaging or an immediate response. Those who responded to my survey were clear about their expectations here. For them, real time could be any period between that same day to 48 hours later.

Third, the ability to send one message to multiple parties aligns with the nature of executive roles, where there are teams of direct and indirect reports. The ease with which executives can relate corporate or division-specific information to their teams is an unequivocal benefit to this group.

Fourth, we appreciate the fact that e-mail can provide paper records of previous decisions, directions, and instructions. We do not attribute this benefit to tracking someone else's work deliverables or lack thereof, but rather we regard this as a tool for recalling past decisions or prior recorded actions for verification at a later date. This positive use of e-mail's tracking capabilities flies in the face of the more insidious and unproductive practice of documenting every action and request by e-mail.

Fifth, we consider the ability to transfer data and information quickly and easily a tremendous benefit to workflows. E-mail and its attachment capability have increased the speed with which information can flow through a work environment. This is especially true when a meeting or telephone conversation occurs that makes reference to more detailed data. By the time the meeting or the call ends, the data may be waiting in our inboxes, while our minds are still fresh from the underlying discussion.

This chapter built a foundation for effective communication by looking not at the words themselves, but at the ways we choose to communicate them. The power of the channel had been fading when, thanks to e-mail, there has been a reversal of fortune, where now the words seem to matter less than the channel itself. Although, as we have seen, the e-mail channel has its own limitations for delivering certain types of content.

There is no doubt that information technology has created levels of processing power and efficiency that were unimaginable even a decade ago. The social changes information technology has created are awe-inspiring and have verified McLuhan's theory of technological determinism many times over. What the e-mail channel has certainly proved beyond a doubt is that the communication tools we shape definitely have a way of shaping us!

Our next chapter, "The Inbox," will show you how to define and shape the e-mail channel for its best uses.

CHAPTER 4

The Inbox

In March 2002, I met with the president of a large multinational firm, who was quite concerned that the use of e-mail had reached epidemic proportions within his firm. Clearly, something had happened to precipitate his call to me. A few minutes into the conversation, I asked him what it was.

His business is such that he is constantly on the move and out of the office for weeks at a time. As a result, he uses his laptop and the telephone to stay in touch with his office. It goes without saying that his laptop is his lifeline to the company.

On a trip to Indonesia, he became separated from his laptop for nearly three days. When he finally got it back and dialed in to his office e-mail, he had 290 messages in his inbox. He realized that this number was completely overwhelming and took action—he deleted all the messages. He did this for two reasons: first, he could not understand why he should receive so many e-mail messages in the first place, and second, he wanted to see how many senders would follow up with him after not receiving his response. Only two people did.

WHY IS THERE SO MUCH E-MAIL?

This story goes to the very root of the workplace e-mail problem—why are we sending so much e-mail to begin with? If we all decided to send fewer e-mails each day, a large portion of the stress we experience in the workplace would diminish.

During the course of my research, I asked people what they disliked most about e-mail in the workplace. Overwhelmingly, the most popular answer was that there is simply too much of it. Clearly, there is a strong sentiment that we need to stop sending most of the messages we are sending. This thinking is exacerbated in particular with executive inboxes that overflow with useless, low-level information. Those people who received over 80 e-mails per day on average simply deleted the hundreds of unread messages every couple of months.

Another related complaint people have is that e-mail is improperly used for all manner of communication, which contributes to the excessive amount we receive. Again, users decide that it is more expeditious to send an e-mail rather than to take the time to converse via telephone or face-to-face. Because e-mail is largely impersonal, it does not build the kind of human connectivity that we need in our workplaces.

The second most popular answer to what people disliked about e-mail is overuse of the reply-to-all and cc features. My research shows that users' frustration with this abuse has grown more intense over the past few years. The biggest problem cited with use of these features was the time it took to understand why they were sent the message at all. In most cases, the knowledge gained was not worth the effort.

These issues lead to the increasing belief that e-mail is now taking too much time to manage. Rather than merely enhancing the exchange of knowledge, e-mail has become an electronic device that imposes additional management responsibilities on us. Increasingly, we can see the irony in a so-called productivity tool that has mutated into an unproductive time thief.

DIFFERENT PERCEPTIONS ABOUT E-MAIL MANAGEMENT

In the past few years, and especially since we've had the technological capability to send attachments, e-mail volumes have increased dramatically. There has been a growing sense that e-mail is dominating workplace communication. For some people—*net-senders*—this was welcome news, as they could exercise more control over their work routines. Sending electronic messages, rather than playing telephone tag or waiting around for a meeting to commence, is actually quite productive. It is even more so if the medium suits the message, and if the information is relevant to the receiver and is structured in a comprehensible, easy-to-read format.

For other employees, workplace e-mail has become just another task to manage. Furthermore, it's a big task that is difficult to ignore. Given the responsibilities and priorities that these individuals already have, e-mail takes on a low priority. Because of time constraints, these people give cursory glances to many e-mail messages, responding only when it's absolutely necessary. These people are *net-receivers,* spending more and more time hunting and pecking through their inboxes for relevant information. For them, e-mail is an unproductive channel for the most part, but a necessary part of the work routine that they must do battle with so that it doesn't overly encroach on their lives. For instance, when asked whether they used remote e-mail devices, many responded quickly that they hoped never to have that level of connectivity. Such sentiments were expressed over and over again, indicating that we have a long way to go to resolving some of e-mail's fundamental problems.

On the other hand, some high-volume users reported being so addicted to using their Blackberry to manage their flow all day long, whether during meetings, in elevators, or in transit, that at some high-level meetings, a basket would be passed around collecting e-mail devices so everyone in the room could disarm themselves from temptation. People are finding other methods to cope with the volume, including what I call "communication multitasking"—where people answer telephone calls while simultaneously responding to a few e-mails.

Most of us fit somewhere in between these two, trying our best to deal with what we perceive as an e-mail onslaught. We talk about this issue with friends and trusted coworkers but often wonder whether we are the only ones who see e-mail volume as a problem. Perhaps we have some personal deficiency or weakness that prevents us from managing e-mail in a better way. "My department or organization doesn't seem to think that there is a problem—no one has raised it as an issue—maybe I'm part of the problem." This may be true, but after exploring the problems and solutions in this book, you should be able to be a champion of e-mail management.

Our perceptions of electronic communication are as varied as our approaches to e-mail management. For this reason, it is almost inconceivable to create that magic bullet, that one-size-fits-all solution for e-mail users. Entities that promise these types of solutions just don't know our reality. E-mail habits and volumes are driven by a variety of underlying causes, as are our reactions. Let's take a closer look at some of them.

WHAT ISSUES ARE CONTRIBUTING TO THE PROBLEM?

Range of contacts, more than recipient's seniority, determines volume of e-mail received. A common perception in the workplace is that the more senior the recipient's rank within the organization, the more e-mails he or she receives. Fifty percent of those receiving 50 or more e-mails per day were managers, not executives. It was the breadth of an individual's role that most determined e-mail volume. In contrast, some senior executives who received 25 e-mails per day still could not respond to them within 24 hours because of their meeting or travel schedules.

Because, as one survey respondent phrased it, "people abuse the privilege of knocking on your door with e-mail," many recipients judge e-mails in terms of their context. If a book is judged by its cover, the same is true for e-mail, whether individuals turn on their inbox preview capability or open the mail directly. E-mail receivers have become very wary, particularly those with higher volumes. Initially, prior to deciding whether to read e-mails, receivers judge them for their relative merits: Is this something that I should review? What will I find when I focus on its content? Clearly, receivers spend time thinking about what they can expect when they open their messages. Their ability to discern the nature of the message at this early stage decides the predisposition toward the message and how they will act on it.

E-mail creates greater stress for the recipient than for the sender. As we have seen throughout the book, effective communication produces a shared understanding between sender and receiver. Sadly, with e-mail, this is often not the case, and respondents seem weary of wrestling with incomprehensible messages. A balance needs to be restored so that receivers do not feel that they have to duck for cover when e-mails come poring in.

The major cause of e-mail stress is its inappropriate use as a communication tool, not its volume. As we have seen, e-mail is replacing other forms of communication, such as informal chats in office corridors, telephone calls, short meetings, lunches with colleagues, longer meetings. My research also revealed that people miss the human touch in their work environments.

Perhaps use of e-mail in the workplace has gone too far for too long, unchecked as to its relative productivity and its corresponding stress levels. A simple calculation using 1.23 hours per day (the overall average additional time spent on e-mail) times 5 days a week for 52 weeks equals 320 hours per year of *extra* time per person devoted to e-mail. For many organizations, this effort does not appear to involve extra costs because many employees are paid by contract or annual salary. Imagine if salaried workers could ask for overtime pay for this extra work; questions might have been asked sooner. But these are some of the extra hours that salaried workers put in as career investments. Imagine an organization that could harness just a portion of this extra time and energy toward productive and creative corporate endeavors—this seems like a scenario that would positively reflect on the bottom line.

How Has Increasing E-mail Volume Impacted Users and the Bottom Line?

Research shows that e-mail has lengthened the work day. Seventy percent of respondents reported spending an average of one extra hour per day on e-mails—an incremental increase over the past two years. For those who receive 50 or more electronic messages per day, the average is 1.5 hours per day. This figure represents a hidden cost for both workers and their organizations. The cost is hidden simply because this extra effort is not highly visible—it is often performed away from the office, usually at home, and it is borne personally by employees. To quote one respondent, "My ex-wife used to ask me, 'When are you ever off work?'" As e-mail from the office makes its way onto the home front, the proper balance of work and quality of life becomes more difficult to maintain. This constant tension, created through connectivity, cannot easily be measured in dollars, nor can its long-term impact. What value would employees place on spending five extra hours per week in personal pursuits? Most of us would surely like the opportunity to find out.

While e-mail volume has gone up, people seem to be finding ways to cope with it to reduce their stress. Not surprisingly, 25 percent of those respondents who were queried on their use of remote e-mail devices use a Blackberry. Sadly, 60 percent of the people surveyed "dial-up" the Sunday before a workweek or periodically during their vacation. Thirty-seven percent take their laptop with them on vacation, with the 50+ group topping this list, at 45 percent. Many respondents said that the alternative—thinking about those e-mails piling up in their inboxes—intruded on their ability to enjoy their vacation. These coping mechanisms may explain why attitudes toward e-mail use have shifted, particularly in the high volume groups— they are forcing a greater degree of connectivity on a continual basis year round.

At the same time, the extra hours logged by employees may appear to be a corporate benefit, but they actually create hidden losses for organizations because employees spend too much time on unproductive matters, with their concentration being siphoned away from more profitable concerns. The opportunity costs are estimated to be in the millions of dollars per year for organizations with several hundred e-mail users. It is doubtful whether this extra five to eight hours per week for 70 percent of employees created a similar incremental increase in the bottom line.

My research showed the growing frustration with e-mail; the correlation between two questions—"How many e-mails do you receive at work daily?" and "Do you think e-mail communication at work is out of control?"—led to my conviction that e-mail volume has become a major problem.

The more e-mails a person received daily, the more adamant they were that electronic mail at the workplace was out of control. Though this may seem obvious after the fact, it is important to note the strong connection between these two answers, and subsequent studies validated this relationship. In fact, 75 percent of people who received between 30 to 49 e-mails a day felt that it was out of control, and 80 percent of people who get 50 or more e-mails a day were firm in this view. These respondents expressed frustration and hostility at the onslaught of incoming messages, and over the two-year study, it became clear that the frustration levels were building.

Where Do We Begin to Solve the Problem?

While the overall problem of e-mail volume is fairly easy to identify, the causes are not as apparent. Given the number and variety of users, we have a complex web of issues to address.

There is no one solution that will work for all users. Some initiatives will have a huge impact, while others will create small victories.

If, however, organizations and individuals use some of the methods we have outlined to combat the problem of too much e-mail, there will be some meaningful results. The most critical step is to create awareness that a problem exists and that it is costing firms millions of dollars every year. In Chapter 1, we debunked the myth that using e-mail is profitable by quantifying the potential annual cost of e-mail overload to an organization with 1,000 employees who are receiving 50+ e-mails per day as over $7 million. This figure is actually higher because it doesn't account for the intangible costs of stress and demotivation.

E-mail problems are rarely topics for strategic discussion among managers. Sometimes e-mail issues flash across corporate radar screens when, for example, the system shuts down because of a sudden flood of reply-to-all e-mails. Once the problem is resolved, however, the issue disappears and the matter is quickly forgotten.

I heard about an interesting incident in a government office. This particular group had been having discussions about resolving e-mail issues to the point of thinking of "e-mail—free days" to create awareness of the problem and take action. During the planning stages, a strike occurred and the workers were off the job for nearly two months. After the strike ended, I received a call from a manager who said that they were going to defer the e-mail initiative because people were too busy trying to reconnect with one another after their long absence.

What is obvious from this story is how critical a communication tool e-mail has become in our workplace. It binds us to our coworkers and our organizations. Of the hundreds of people with whom I have spoken about e-mail, there was not one person who wanted to do without it in the workplace. Most people cannot imagine an efficient work environment without e-mail. As most of us now know only too well, sheer volume is not the biggest problem. The noise or static that our inboxes capture is. By noise, I refer to those e-mails that are not relevant or essential to our jobs. It is almost like listening to a radio that is not exactly set on the station—we hear the music, but we hear it over the static. We must concentrate that much harder to discern the music over the static and this requires more of our mental energies . . . until, of course, we decide to change to a clearer station.

We do not have the luxury of changing our inboxes, however. We have to make changes from within. According to my research, most people manage their inboxes in the following ways:

Scanning:	82 percent
First in, first out:	15 percent
Last in, first out:	3 percent

We tend to select e-mail items in the following order: urgent flags, by sender, by topic, by date sent.

We also tend to devise our own methods for coping with the messages in our inboxes. How would you deal with one hundred new e-mail messages? Many people use the following methods:

1. *Quickly scan through all the new e-mails to get a sense of the nature of their content.* Take mental note of those messages that look like a series of related items, as well as those messages that you think can be deleted because they are low value. These include all those dreadful spam messages!

2. *Delete all the low-value messages.* Don't be curious about that unrecognizable new address that appears—chances are highly likely that it is external spam. Also keep in mind that if you see a message with an address that you don't recognize and the message includes an attachment, a virus may be lurking. This is all the more reason to delete the message immediately. If you make deleting these messages a habit, approximately 30 percent of the messages in your inbox should disappear every day.

3. *Focus on those series of messages that relate to one particular topic.* Read the first message if you need a refresher, and then read the last one or the most recent one sent. Using this strategy should help inform you about an

issue and you should be able to delete the remaining messages on this topic.

By now your inbox should be about 60 percent of its original size (these three steps should have taken 10 minutes maximum). Take another quick scan to see what else can be deleted and what should be printed for later reading or review.

Now that your inbox is more manageable, turn on the preview pane feature, if you use it, and deal with the most important messages in the following order—messages from your superiors, then key clients, then subordinates.

Following these steps may help you to quickly manage 100 new e-mail messages (or more) quite painlessly. Do you feel uneasy about deleting unread e-mail messages? It is important to keep in mind that low-relevance messages are major time eaters, especially if you need to spend time thinking about what to do with some of your other e-mail messages. If your time is at a premium, it's best to make a conscious effort to delete e-mails that do not impact you. Even if you accidentally delete an important message, it is not a fatal error. If people need information from you, they will get it through another communication channel, or send you another e-mail message.

LOW-VALUE MESSAGES THAT CLOG OUR INBOXES

There are several types of common messages that routinely clog our inboxes. They are spam, messages addressed to distribution lists within an organization, and what I like to call *e-mail Ping-Pong*—those short message relay matches that seem to go on indefinitely.

Spam

A major source of clogged inboxes is workplace *spam*. Spam—a cyber term that refers to unsolicited bulk e-mail—is a huge problem for e-mail users, especially home users. According to the Federal Trade Commission, which tracks spam through specially segregated e-mail addresses, volume tripled in 2002. Consumers are seeking legal remedies, with which the Commission has some influence, and new companies that create antispamming technologies have arrived on the scene. So far, though, it appears that the spammers are winning the battle. We can only hope that the enactment of national legislation with some real teeth will eventually eradicate spam from our inboxes.

Company firewalls and filters block out a great deal of spam traffic, but some messages still manage to get through. People receive an average of 14 pieces of external, unsolicited bulk mail per week. This is an excellent result when you realize that your personal electronic inbox at home may easily receive this many in a single day. However, the workplace is not entirely free of spam—some of it just takes on a different form and causes more ongoing frustration because it is not always so obvious. This book will help you alleviate some of the problems spam causes; for now, let us simply identify some of the workplace spam sources you might encounter. Learning to recognize these offenders is essential to effective inbox management. Here are some classifications of workplace spam I devised for purposes of differentiation.

Intuition spam:	Messages sent by well-intentioned coworkers who intuit that you will want to see a particular message—they loved it, and so will you! Items in this category include chain mail, jokes, and those "fabulous" web-links full of information that you won't be able to live without.
Writing spam:	The poorly planned, poorly conceived message that holds readers hostage and does not let them go until they've spent too much time trying to determine what it means. These also include those spurious e-mails that find their way into our inboxes. You know the ones—cc's, replies-to-all, and those blow-by-blow accounts of how every minute of every day was spent. It is like stepping into quicksand and struggling to climb back out.
Profile spam:	These e-mails are contrived by the sender to make sure that the receiver is keeping the sender in mind. It does not matter about the content of the message. In fact, this may be cleverly disguised. The prime intention of this type of spam is to manipulate this channel to achieve career advancement through greater personal visibility.
Friendly spam:	This category of messages includes personal requests for donations, identifying items for sale and virtually anything one person can broadcast to many.
Corporate spam:	Messages that originate from a variety of well-meaning internal departments who want to make certain that they have informed everybody on mission-critical information. Examples include "the Finance department will all be out to lunch

today," "the bathroom facilities on the 28th floor are flooded," and "the server is down."

Commercial spam:	Messages from associations, vendors, and would-be suppliers—people who want to do business with you or have done so in the past. You have purchased something or expressed an interest in a new office item or dropped your business card at a trade show and you are forever on their mailing lists.
Camouflage spam:	Messages that are carefully and clinically documented notes disguised as e-mails. Some employees with too much time on their hands or who fear verbal exchanges will use e-mail to transcribe and record conversations. Sometimes these employees will store the messages in their electronic file folders, but more often, they will send these messages to relevant recipients after attending a conversation or meeting, solely to protect themselves.

Internal Distribution Lists

Although messages that are sent to those recipients who are on distribution lists do not fit within the spam category, they come close. The problems with distribution lists are not who is on the lists, but how the lists are used and managed. These following scenarios are common and among the more annoying e-mail messages people receive in the workplace:

1. There are 280 people on an association's distribution list. Twenty-three members still owe dues. An e-mail

goes out to everyone asking those who have not paid to do so.

2. Twenty people serve on a task force. An e-mail inquires about their availability to attend an optional function. Nine people respond that they can attend, and the remaining 11 send their regrets. Subsequent e-mails on the event continue to go out to all 20 people.

3. An individual receives a promotion at work and is transferred from the finance department in one city to the legal department in another. She still continues to receive group notices from her former department.

4. Although most firms discourage personal use of corporate distribution lists in favor of posting information on the corporate Intranet, there is always someone who posts "Computer for sale" or "Cookies for sale" or "Please donate" over the e-mail system.

There is no doubt that distribution lists and the ability to send the same message simultaneously to several (or many hundred) individuals is one of e-mail's tremendous benefits. However, this capability is abused to the point where its benefits are overshadowed. Many of us find our inboxes littered with messages that we should not be receiving, causing a great deal of frustration.

There are three distinct problems that occur with distribution lists. First, messages intended for the few are sent to the many. In most of these cases, these lists help people within specific departments to execute and complete a task. They use lists when they require a response, and this is where the problem lies. It is so convenient to press the send button, scatter a message throughout work groups, and wait for the responses. After all, this is the intention of e-mail communication. But for some individuals who receive this message, it has absolutely no relevance and they spend more time than needed to keep the volume of their inboxes under control.

Second, departments use distribution lists to send news and information to all employees. Messages can proliferate from any number of departments including finance, human resources, information technology, executive management, and operations. As a rule, these messages do not require a response. In April 2000, the *New York Times* reported the story of a CEO who e-mailed his 30,000 employees and invited their responses. The weight of the responses crashed his office e-mail system.

Many messages sent via distribution lists are important to employees, but they must have communication value or employees won't read them. Stories abound in some industries about global "all-employee" messages that are too long (more than four screens), use a demeaning tone (i.e., "They did it, why can't you?"), and are not relevant to a particular group of employees.

In addition, how many times do you see managers forwarding the same message, accompanied at times with their personal commentary? Conceptually, this is one way to take advantage of e-mail's benefit for reaching multiple parties with the same message. It backfires, however, when employees start receiving multiple forwards of messages that they have already read and discarded. Now all they perceive is inefficiency, not good communication.

Third, distribution lists, like web sites and corporate Intranets, need constant management. People move around in organizations, and, as they do, departmental distribution lists need to be updated. The lists also must be purged of e-mail addresses that are no longer valid.

In my research, I asked the question: "What types of e-mails would you love to return to sender?" Here are the most popular answers:

- Low-level information from distribution lists
- Unsolicited e-mails from vendors and suppliers
- CC, reply-to-all and FYI e-mails

Interestingly, these responses all relate to distribution lists of one sort or another. The only difference is the source. It seems obvious that many of us do not like being on someone's list especially when we never granted permission to be on the list in the first place. Indeed, many of us are infuriated at the seeming injustice of these lists—our name gets on all too easily, but we cannot be removed from a list without some effort.

Some of us do try to be removed from lists, but the results can be mixed. In one case I'm aware of, an e-mail had been sent to a group of past and present business associates. The context of the e-mail had angered one of the recipients and he asked that he be removed from the list. The sender proceeded to address his rather caustic remarks on this request and distributed the message to everyone on the list, which caused a lot more grief.

However they are constructed, distribution lists require much consideration, planning, and management. It may only be a matter of time before enough people grumble long and hard enough to put a stop to the practice. In one successful instance, a department head asked to be removed from an all-employee list citing that the information received via the list had absolutely no relevance to his position. This action caused a review of this department's practices and relevant new and smaller lists were created as a result.

Solutions

Let's revisit the scenarios to frame some solutions:

The first scenario involves a decision on whether to use a large distribution list to reach a small group within it. Do not use a distribution list to reach less than 80 percent of the intended audience. Sending to all may save time for the sender, but it definitely wastes time for the majority of the people on the list who merely delete the message. If the list cannot be modified easily, then create another, smaller list.

The second scenario relates to the management of a subset of a small distribution list for a specific purpose. Once people have decided that they are not interested in this information, create a separate distribution list of those people who are, and continue to correspond with them. People appreciate focused communication, but not superfluous updates.

In the third scenario, a transferred employee keeps receiving e-mail from her previous department. Remove employees from distribution lists when they transfer or leave the company, and periodically update distribution lists.

The fourth scenario involves individuals who want to sell or collect something and decide to bypass the corporate Intranet. E-mail policies that discourage this practice are one way to remind employees that corporate time and equipment should not be put to personal use. Reinforcing the policy, especially when infractions occur, is also effective.

E-mail has certainly helped bridge a part of the communication gap that many employees feel, but it is not the total solution. Using a combination of all communication channels and keeping the information relevant and focused is essential. That being said, there are several ways that organizations and individuals can improve the management of these types of messages:

- Keep messages short and to the point; provide an executive summary (one screen long) of crucial information on an e-mail and refer employees to the corporate Intranet for details. Such a quick briefing will engage only those employees who wish to know more.

- Review practices for sending all-employee e-mail to take into account corporate hierarchy and chains of command. In other words, give managers the opportunity to manage by considering using distribution lists at the managerial level, so that managers can add their commentary and forward those messages they think are important to their employees. There will always be messages that need to go out to all employees from one source, but there are probably other types of messages—relating perhaps to organizational changes—that affect employees, where the chain-of-command technique for e-mail distribution will enhance communication for all parties concerned.

- Do not forward all-employee messages unless you are certain that there were groups left out of the original distribution. Field sales representatives who are working on remote computers with slower processing speeds don't appreciate receiving four or five large, identical messages.

- Consider controlling access to all-employee and/or other large distribution lists. E-mail is a valuable corporate resource and managing it well can enhance employee productivity. Giving everyone ready access to large distribution lists is similar to making confidential information available to all employees. There are perfectly valid reasons for controlling information within organizations. Why not extend the same vigilance to a mechanism for distributing information?

- Ask to be removed from distribution lists that you don't need to be on.

- Manage e-mail distribution lists as you would meetings and other personal interactions. Communicate only with those individuals who have expressed a continued need-to-know for further information. Remember that distribution lists are dynamic and require constant updating to keep them current.

- Don't intrude on your coworkers' time and space by using corporate distribution lists for your personal causes (no matter how noble). Use lunchroom or common areas (which include Intranets) to post your personal requests. Your coworkers will be grateful for the reprieve.

E-mail Ping-Pong

There are times that we can get trapped in our use of e-mail to accomplish tasks. The trap gets set when we try to use e-mail in a synchronous manner—like a running dialogue. As we saw in Chapter 3's example of the Lawson file, e-mail was being used to replace a brief conversation on locating a file. The problem in this example was the choice of e-mail as the most efficient channel for communication. With e-mail Ping-Pong, we take this a step further in our deliberate attempts to commit ourselves to additional e-mail cycles.

What characterizes these cycles is their ability to extend the life of an e-mail transmission, and their relative low value as information. This may not be workplace spam, but it certainly comes close. Many survey respondents lamented over these types of practices. The two most commonly cited ones—meeting requests and tagged-on social graces—are highlighted next.

The Problem with Meetings

Could we meet in the next few days?

Sure, what time is good for you?

How about this Thursday? Are you free for lunch?

No, I'm booked. I have some free time at 3:00 P.M.

Sorry, I'm not available then. Would 10:00 A.M. that day work?

No, I've got an offsite client meeting. How about next week?

This is a typical example of e-mail Ping-Pong—communication that can go on forever. Messages like this serve only to clog our inboxes and consume our time. E-mail is an inanimate way of communicating—it is words on a screen, a nonverbal transmission. Nevertheless, we keep trying to humanize e-mail and to force it into the realm of our interactive communication channels—the telephone and face-to-face.

This Ping-Pong e-mail example is yet another classic situation where electronic mail is not a good substitute for live interaction. Six e-mails have been exchanged, and nothing has been resolved. The meeting date and time are not yet imminent, and this situation could continue for another six e-mails. This situation and others like it are blatant time wasters. Clicking away at the keyboard may seem productive, but in terms of the time we spend receiving, reading, and responding to these low-value messages, the company has already more than paid for our lunch.

To avoid this pitfall, consider what you are trying to achieve by initiating an e-mail message and whether you will accomplish your communication goal within one mail cycle (send once, receive once). If you cannot easily achieve this objective, use the telephone. If the telephone is not feasible or is too costly, then write a high-content e-mail message to speed the process along. Using our scenario above as an example, a high-content e-mail cycle may be expressed as follows:

Could we meet in the next few days? I'm open this Thursday and Friday for lunch or in the afternoons.

Sure, I'm not available for lunch on either day but would 2:00 P.M. on Friday suit you?

Yes. I'll see you at your office.

In three e-mails, they achieved game, set, and match.

Acknowledgments

E-mail from Helena to the consulting team: We are getting together for an end of project party. Don't miss the excitement. See you there on Friday night.

This message does not ask for a response, yet these are the types of responses that will be sent:

From consultant A to Helena: Thanks for letting me know.

From consultant B to Helena: Just letting you know that I'll be arriving late.

From consultant C to Helena and the entire consulting team: Unfortunately, I'll be unable to attend.

From consultant D to Helena and the entire consulting team: I'm leaving for Singapore the next morning, but I'll try to be there.

These response messages can now spawn additional Ping-Pong e-mails such as:

From Helena to consultant A: You're welcome.

From consultant B to consultant C and the entire consulting team: If D can try to be there, why can't you?

Etc., etc., etc.

Sending acknowledgments back and forth is another variety of the Ping-Pong trap. Given the demands for greater formality in workplace e-mail, rules of courtesy remain somewhat uncertain, as do expectations about response. Many people acknowledge e-mails on receipt, especially if they are unable to respond in detail for a day or two. Still others send "Thank you" e-mails to acknowledge their pleasure at a response, which encourages a "You're welcome" response, and once more, we are playing another game of Ping-Pong communication. To reduce our daily e-mail traffic to only those items that are relevant, we should all agree to curtail these types of courtesies.

Sending a "Thank you" e-mail message for receiving a response or receiving certain information is usually not necessary and serves merely to clog the receiver's inbox. On the reverse side, many people do not expect a detailed response but they are waiting for us to send them a "Thank you." When they don't get it, they somehow feel slighted and this can create tension in our future interactions with the individual. To reduce the potential for this kind of tension, you can actually build courtesies into the body of your e-mail message. People have often asked me about the right way to start and end an e-mail. This is what I suggest: When appropriate, use a greeting for your e-mails, such as:

Hello _____ (Use the person's first name if you know it or Mr./Ms./Dr. if you are writing to someone for the first time.)

Hi

Greetings

Only their first name, if you know them well

[Nothing at all as in the standard written memo format]

If it is appropriate, you can close the e-mail by thanking them in advance for their assistance. Always close your e-mail messages with one of the following:

Regards,

Cheers,

Sincerely,

[Your first name or first and last name if you need to keep the message formal]

Refrain from sending acknowledgment or thank-you e-mails. Assume the e-mail has been delivered. If you do choose to send a "Thank you," then save it for when you wish to express an additional opinion or thought. If you feel strongly that it's really important to thank someone, then using the telephone or stopping by that person's office is the better choice.

Referring to our previous scenario, the e-mail from Helena did not request any acknowledgment, so don't supply one by e-mail—thank her in person at the office party instead. This type of personal gesture will most certainly be appreciated.

USING E-MAIL WISELY

There are many ways we can manage our outbound messages in an effort to control electronic mail volume. First, for every e-mail message that you plan to send, ask yourself why you are sending the message in the first place. Are you copying your boss on e-mails to impress him or her, or to avoid making decisions? Do you copy everyone who may be concerned about an issue, to ensure "plausible deniability" if ever your actions are called into question? There are some details that people just don't need to know. You might be saying to yourself, "Oh well, if they don't want the information, they can just delete it." Although recipients can do just that, why take up their time?

The act of deleting e-mail requires careful consideration. We can quickly delete some e-mail if we are aware of its contents—this usually happens with auto-e-mail, regularly sent corporate messages, and vendor or supplier push e-mails. For the remaining messages, the *art of deleting* is not automatic. We won't know whether to delete a message until we actually open and quickly scan its contents. At that point, we may decide to delete it. This deletion process could take up to five minutes for each e-mail. Therefore, if you are receiving a dozen of these "just delete if not important" e-mails, you are spending about an hour each day struggling through low-value information that you should never have received to begin with (and wouldn't have, if electronic mail were not available).

When you send e-mail, consider your audience. E-mail should be receiver-centered, not sender-centered. In other words, only send e-mail if your intended receivers can act on the information and it is within the scope of their work duties.

Although one of our favorite features of e-mail is the ability to send the same message to multiple parties, this is also a feature we tend to abuse. You should copy e-mail only to those individuals who need the information. If you are dealing with a group of 10 people, and only six of them require more information or details, send the information to only those six. If you believe it's necessary to copy a senior individual into the situation, do so only if you have permission from that person. Many executives have told me that there is nothing more disconcerting than suddenly being copied in on an ongoing situation and having to take time out of their busy work day to understand why.

Using e-mail's blind corresponding copy (bcc) feature has also become an unbridled practice in many organizations. This feature enables employees to send and receive e-mail and directly copy it to other parties without the original sender being aware of it. Before e-mail, people were prudent in their use of the bcc feature with paper memos. E-mail users are now using this feature more often, and it is causing greater alarm in the workplace by feeding people's paranoia that they might be monitored or judged without their knowledge or consent.

Do not use the reply-to-all feature unless you are fully convinced that the information you are relaying is of vital importance to all the people on your e-mail list. Most people use this feature unintentionally—just because the button resides beside the "reply" button on most e-mail message screens does not mean that it has a similar function. This button is not a link to a chat line. It is critical to ask yourself whether 30 people on a list really need to know your response or your thoughts—if not, always reply just to the original sender.

While e-mail is cheap, easy to use, and easy to access for just about anyone in the world, it is first and foremost a formal communication channel in the workplace. As such, we need to use it with the same type of consideration that we would practice in a face-to-face, team, or client meeting.

PRACTICAL TOOLS TO HELP REDUCE YOUR PERSONAL E-MAIL VOLUME

If you are like most people, you probably did not receive any formal e-mail training. The application was installed and virtually ready to go. Years have gone by, and you still wonder whether you know enough about managing your e-mail application. You are not alone. From my discussions with workshop and seminar participants, there are still a few of you out there who are not certain how to physically remove messages from your inboxes once you've dealt with them. Many of you have discovered how to operate your e-mail applications only through trial and error and discussion with colleagues. Most of you wish you had a bit more knowledge.

This section covers some of the basic utilities that exist in e-mail software packages that can help you manage your inbound and outbound messages. The most common office e-mail software packages are Eudora, Group Wise, Lotus Notes, and Microsoft Outlook. The functions covered next are available on most of the newer versions of these packages, especially the junk e-mail filters, but you will probably find these functions under various menu selections and perhaps their names will be different. The general information will provide you with greater awareness of e-mail applications and some of their key functions. Remember that each program will be a little different so get comfortable with the program you use.

Functions for Managing Incoming Messages

You can't control the content or length of the messages you receive in your inbox. What you can do, however, is use your e-mail application to help you organize your incoming messages and in some cases, quickly ascertain their content to determine their significance. The following are some of the functions that can help you do that.

Preview Pane

Preview pane displays the first few lines of incoming e-mail on your inbox screen so that you can scan a message quickly to ascertain its content and level of importance. When you use this feature, the sender cannot determine whether you've read the message or even opened the message. However, the preview pane feature does consume space on your inbox screen and forces you to scroll through more screens.

Color Coding

Some e-mail packages permit you to set both color coding and font changes for different types of incoming messages. For example, messages from specific people or sources can appear in different colors from other types of messages. You might use this function to separate messages that are addressed personally to you from corresponding copy (cc) messages. Alternatively, you might separate messages such as auto-generated and distribution list information from your more routine e-mail traffic. Your use of this feature depends on whether color coding and font changes help you prioritize incoming e-mail.

Folders

Directing inbound messages automatically to electronic filing folders rather than having them all appear on the inbox screen is a useful organizational function. For example, you could divert all auto-generated messages like newsletters or the contents of internal distribution lists. This can help you separate reading material from your day-to-day work messages.

Folders also help you organize messages once you've handled them. You don't need to keep every message, but there may be circumstances when it is helpful to create an electronic file that you can refer to rather than printing selected messages and storing them in your office filing cabinet. It is possible to create as many files as you need and to separate handled or pending items from your current e-mail. Subfolders can facilitate a finer degree of sorting by subject. In addition, you can drag and drop dated messages from your inbox into your designated folders. Like paper files, you should review and "clean" your electronic folders periodically.

Junk Mail Filter

This filter permits you to block mail that comes from specific addresses. However, you can usually only apply this feature, after you've received an unwanted message. At that point, you can assign all other mail from this address directly to the junk-mail file. For the mail that originates from multiple addresses, corporate firewalls and filters are already working to keep them out of your system. The junk-mail filter gives you a little more control over unwanted messages that regularly show up in your inbox.

Out-of-Office Assistant

The out-of-office assistant tool automatically advises people who are sending you e-mail that you are not in the office and won't be able to respond to their e-mail within a certain time frame. Using this feature, you can create a customized message that instructs people to contact someone else or otherwise advises them of your contact status. While this feature does not stop e-mail messages from collecting in your inbox, it at least alleviates some of the pressure that you might feel when you leave your office for a few days and won't have access to your e-mail system.

Functions for Managing Outgoing Messages

Although you cannot directly control the content and length of the messages you receive, you do have control over the messages you send. You control their content and you control their length. You can also use your e-mail application to make your messages easier for your recipients to read. The following functions can help you manage your outbound messages more efficiently.

Standard Fonts

Most e-mail software packages permit a great deal of individual customization. For instance, you can adjust font types, sizes, and colors. To promote comprehension, it's best to use standard, serif fonts such as Times Roman and Courier because serif fonts make it easier for people to read sentences and paragraphs. (A serif is a fine line that's visible on the main strokes of a letter as at the top and bottom of the letter N.) Font size should be no less than 10 points and no more than 12 points. Type that is larger or smaller makes the e-mail messages more difficult for the recipient to read.

The best text color to use is black (because most screens have light or white backgrounds), but other dark colors like blue offer sufficient contrast for easy reading.

Auto Signature

The auto signature provides all your contact information and appears at the end of every outgoing message. This is an excellent feature that saves the receiver time in finding your contact details. The auto signature does not replace a personal sign-off, whether it is "Regards" or "Sincerely," but it does deliver the same kind of information as paper-based letterhead—full name, title, return e-mail address, and phone numbers. Some auto signatures include full mailing addresses, which is appropriate if a general audience may need to correspond with the sender via surface (*snail*) mail. The key here is to be efficient and sensible about what you include in your signature.

For instance, do not make the signature an attachment that the receiver can simply add to her or his address book. This assumes that everyone keeps an automated address file and that your name should go in there if they do. Do not create graphically intense or overly large-font auto signatures. I have seen some signatures that take up a half screen or more. With auto signatures, size does matter: smaller and simpler signatures are more professional and easier to read.

Sent Message Folder

The sent folder contains copies of all the e-mail messages you compose and send. The benefit of this function is that you have a record of the messages you transmit in case a misunderstanding results and you need to verify the accuracy and completeness of the information you originally provided.

Attaching Incoming Messages

This function allows you to decide whether to automatically attach the original message you are responding to within the message you're preparing to send. Many people don't realize that this is an option that they can control. In terms of e-mail management, this feature can be beneficial because usually the content of earlier messages is irrelevant to the current e-mail topic and you don't want readers to waste more valuable time reading earlier messages that are no longer pertinent.

HOW TO REDUCE E-MAIL VOLUME IN YOUR ORGANIZATION

Research shows that over 70 percent of respondents felt strongly that their organization should step in and try to minimize the problems with e-mail. The solution to e-mail problems in the workplace again rest with our ability to answer two questions: "Can we do something about it?" and "Should we?"

Questions surrounding such a monumental task abound, such as "Is it a problem in my department or company?"

"Where exactly is the problem?" "What can I do about this problem, if I cannot control all the outcomes?" The good news is that we can do a great deal with little effort. Resolving workplace e-mail problems is not in the order of magnitude of a large-scale process change or a re-engineering project. It does not require huge amounts of documentation, organizational changes, or new information technology resources. Instead, it requires:

- Awareness of e-mail problems in the workplace
- Corporate energy to resolve the major issues
- Individual attention that sets new standards
- Review and reinforcement for long-term benefits

With individual, small group, and corporate initiatives working in tandem, e-mail frustration can be alleviated in an organization.

INDIVIDUAL AND SMALL GROUP INITIATIVES

We already know what drives us crazy about e-mail practices in the workplace. We need to bring our issues to the attention of management so that they become aware of the problems and their impact on productivity. Information technology, human resources, and public affairs executives have often asked me for advice on how to begin to tackle the e-mail problem in their organizations. One of the first questions that I ask them is about the circumstances that have led them to contact me. Invariably, a senior executive has become acutely aware of the problem due to a personal experience—whether it's receiving a flood of junk e-mail, an e-mail deluge while traveling, or suddenly realizing that receiving 100 messages a day is ridiculous.

Not all awareness has to come from the top. In one multi-national company, a departmental administrator became so offended at a joke that was being circulated on the corporate e-mail system that she took it upon herself to forward the item to human resources with a demand that the department do something. The human resources department developed and circulated a comprehensive, two-page e-mail policy that was widely reinforced.

Regardless of how an e-mail problem is eventually identified, the issue needs a corporate champion or two to take it to the next step. Awareness at any level begins with reviewing your own e-mail practices and determining your own satisfaction with inbox messages. You can expand your awareness by unearthing anecdotal information from your colleagues, superiors, and subordinates.

At this point, you may be asking how you can get started in reducing e-mail volumes today. For those who have achieved awareness, the following six steps provide a quick guide:

1. *Recognition*. Recognize that your department or organization may have an e-mail overload problem that is costing time and money, and evaluate where positive action is possible.

2. *Data gathering*. Use informal surveys and focus groups to turn anecdotal experience into empirical measures.

These tools can offer quantitative perspective on the worst practices regarding e-mail.

3. *Validation.* Validation tests early findings with broader groups in the organization to gather support for the quantitative data.

4. *Planning action.* Seek out more formal corporate support through human resources, corporate communications, or executive management to obtain resources for developing appropriate in-house solutions. Use this as an opportunity to create a communication action plan.

5. *Implementation.* Roll out the initiative on a pilot basis (using one department) and, based on what you learn, refine the implementation.

6. *Measurement.* Establish e-mail measures (i.e., average number per person, ability to respond within standard work hours) as a benchmark that works within the organization. Use these measures to evaluate progress.

CORPORATE INITIATIVES AND SUPPORT

E-mail is a valuable corporate resource that facilitates the distribution and dissemination of information to employees and stakeholders. Just as companies can employ surveillance software to monitor use of their electronic equipment, they must also assume the lead role in pursuit of e-mail excellence. Without a sincere and realistic display of leadership and action in this area, the benefits will be short-lived, if realized at all.

It is unlikely that the CEO and her or his leadership team will become visible spokespeople and disciples for reducing e-mail volume. However, their full support in initiation, along with "walking the walk," is critical. This same type of top-down support is key to any successful initiative that organizations choose to implement.

A suggested starting point is to diagnose the types of e-mail problems that an organization faces from the following perspectives:

Information broadcasts:	From corporate departments to all employees or by department or job function.
Reporting broadcasts:	Quantitative information by type (finance, marketing, sales, operations), their frequency, and the audience reached.
Employee broadcasts:	Initiated by employees—purpose, type of message, and subject matter.
Average volumes:	Average number of daily e-mails received and responded to, by job rank or function.
Relevance:	Relevance of e-mail to both job function and bottom line contribution.
Norms and practices:	A review of how and why senior management initiates and uses e-mail within the workplace (their habits cascade throughout an organization).
Knowledge:	Knowledge of the e-mail system itself (privacy and monitoring concerns), its use as a communication channel, and how to construct messages that communicate objectives clearly.

Data gathering and analysis of these dimensions will provide a good blueprint for the overall issues. This type of exercise also should reveal where simple, quick fixes are possible and what areas require more focus and effort.

What should be the goal in this exercise besides simply reducing e-mail volumes and creating a better communication environment? What kind of measure could we use? I suggest attempting to reduce average e-mail volumes for all job functions to 25 to 30 per day. The benefit in using a number is that research has shown that e-mail problems tend to be more counterproductive and stressful as average daily volumes rise. We've already calculated that the normal rate for e-mail is 25 per day. At this level, the percentage of relevant, job-related e-mail is at its highest, and most people can manage this volume of inbound information on both a quantitative and qualitative basis. Second, a numerical goal permits organizations to measure, over time, the impact of their initiatives.

If a company determines that its average volume at the managerial level is 56 e-mails per day (higher than the current average of 48), it can easily measure the impact of the changes it makes with another sample three or six months later. For example, in three months, a reduction from 56 to 50 messages per day is certainly a move in the right direction, but it is not a major change. This small reduction would be the signal to verify if the enacted changes actually target some of the large-volume issues. If they do not, initiating new and different changes might reduce volume more effectively.

Executives or managers should think about their own e-mail volumes—How many messages are productive and job-related versus nice-to-know push messages? One method of doing this is to use a four-point scale to categorize incoming e-mails by their relevance. Here are some message relevance measurements I have used (from high to low): essential, relevant, not very relevant, and irrelevant. Individuals track their e-mail messages for a week, recording on their tracking sheets the category in which each incoming e-mail belongs. Notice I said what the receiver *believes* to be an essential e-mail versus a junk e-mail. While this belief corresponds with individual tastes, I have found that most people (even those who like receiving chain mail) will invariably log them into the appropriate low relevance categories.

At the end of a week, people have a good handle on the magnitude of their e-mail problem. A next step could be to extend this weeklong categorization to their department to compare notes with others and build an empirical database, potentially developing a case for taking this internal research further.

INDIVIDUAL ATTENTION

If an organization decides to create an e-mail policy to govern the intended uses of the e-mail system, the policy provides employee groups with a framework for their future guidance and management. This policy or set of guiding principles provides a backdrop and a common set of rules, much like the spirit of the corporate code of conduct. It is not "big brother" mandating personal behaviors and choices. Rather, it is a guide to promoting more efficiency and to reducing the time workers devote to sending, reading, and receiving low-value e-mail. A general code that is intended for all employees—including senior executives—and is taken seriously can motivate painless and fruitful change.

To implement a corporation-wide code successfully, managers will need to develop and offer training that will address any gaps of knowledge that exist in e-mail application functions and/or basic composition skills. Training that reduces time and energy spent on e-mail will slash e-mail volumes.

Mention the word *training*, however, and many people are one of two minds—either I need training, or I do not have time to take half a day off for training. For those industries and working groups where large blocks of time for training are not possible, I suggest using a more creative approach, especially as it pertains to educating users about their e-mail application. Develop lists of 5 to 10 electronic mail application functions, writing the explanations in simple, user-friendly language, and circulate these to all employees or post them on the corporate Intranet. Create three or more such lists at varying levels such as basic, intermediate, advanced, and expert. This approach can help users learn about e-mail software functions on their own timetable.

E-mail composition is easier to learn in one- or two-hour workshops, which are supplemented with written course material for the users' future reference. Most people do not mind devoting a couple of hours in a workday to learning about ways to become a more effective communicator. Additionally, managers can use this book to teach and reinforce communication skills within the workplace.

REVIEW AND REINFORCEMENT

Managers should periodically review and address e-mail volumes and practices in the workplace. It takes effort to initiate any type of change that affects an organization and its employees. It also takes effort to monitor the progress of these changes as they begin to take hold within the first year.

This chapter introduced us to a number of common e-mail issues that we face every day, providing valuable solutions and tips that you can incorporate right away. As with the previous chapter, and with the upcoming chapter, this information should be reviewed and discussed often among your colleagues and coworkers. I guarantee you that there will be any number of occasions where something comes up at work that is referenced in these chapters.

In addition, there is a wealth of information in this chapter on how to begin to reduce e-mail volume within your respective departments or organizations. The intent of this information is to provide key points of reference that will make it much easier for you to initiate some fact-finding within your work area. Electronic mail problems are not just single user issues, but are embedded within our organizations as well.

The next chapter focuses on individual needs and shows you how to be a skillful e-mail sender.

CHAPTER

5

The Outbox

Up to this point, we have taken the e-mail receiver's perspective in dealing with many issues surrounding incoming messages. By now you can appreciate the importance
of creating a shared understanding through effective e-mail
structure and content. We also know that too many e-mails are
sent with either low-value information or as a proxy for using a
different communication channel.

No doubt you have embraced many of the ideas within this
book and have put them into practice. At this point, you may
feel very enlightened on inbox management issues, but may
have some concerns on defining your role as an e-mail sender.
To remedy this, we'll first discuss how to manage the time you
spend sending and responding to electronic mail, and you'll
come away with some general guidelines toward better citizen-
ship in this global e-mail village. Then we'll explore message

content—we'll walk you through the essentials of effective communication and provide tips to help you craft messages that are easy to read.

OUTBOX MANAGEMENT

This section maps out the basic components for superior management of outgoing messages. It is divided into two segments—sending and responding.

Initiating an E-mail

When initiating an e-mail, you should ask yourself three questions:

1. What is the purpose of my message?
2. Who should I send it to?
3. Is e-mail the right channel?

This is the planning stage of e-mail. It is the most critical diagnostic of whether you will send an inconsequential or low-value e-mail or the right message. Some time and care should be taken here—it could be anywhere from a few minutes for a more routine matter, to several hours if you find you need more time to think about what it is you want to communicate. Don't be at all surprised if in some instances, after some deliberation, you decide against sending an electronic message altogether. This simply means that you have considered your purpose and decided against either the channel or the audience or both.

What is important here is that each e-mail initiated is done so with confidence and clear intent.

Your audience is another key area. Outside of considering who is the right person for the message, you need to understand his or her knowledge, attitude, and needs. What does she already know about the subject you are addressing? What kind of attitude might she have toward the subject, toward you, and toward incoming e-mails? Does this e-mail fulfill a need felt by the recipient?

If you know your audience well, as in the case of a coworker, you then need to ask yourself whether your message is time sensitive and requires an answer within say, 24 hours. As we have seen, people place differing priorities on e-mail communication. Because most people receive too many e-mails each workday, depending on the individual, electronic mail may not be the best route to obtain a time-sensitive response.

Now you are ready to begin crafting the e-mail message. The three elements you need to consider are developing the subject line, stating the objective of the message, and organizing the content.

As we have seen earlier, the subject line is one of the two most critical parts of an e-mail message. It sets up the reader's expectations and frames their anticipated actions. The other part of e-mail's compositional dynamic duo is the first sentence of the message, or your stated objective. This is where you need to tell your audience what action you want them to take before they read on. Given the close relationship between these two elements, it's best to develop them together.

Once this has been accomplished, you are ready to develop the message content. While we'll explore this in more detail later in this chapter, the key technical aspects to remember here are to keep the message concise—let your subject line and first sentence be your guide. Feel free to use the white space—paragraph breaks, bullet points—to enhance the readability of the message, and try to keep the message including auto-signature to one screen.

The last thing you need to consider are attachments. For some messages, their purpose is to simply forward the attached file—in these cases, the messages should either be very brief or explain where the receiver should focus his attention. In other cases, consider whether the attachment is really a requirement, or whether it could be saved for subsequent correspondence when your audience is expressing an interest in additional information. Too often e-mails bombard their audiences with extraneous, easy-to-attach items, that are rarely opened. Don't fall into this easy habit of sending extra information. It's better to err on the side of brevity.

Before you press send . . .

- Spellcheck your e-mail. Most software packages have an automated feature that you can set either to spellcheck during composition or to initiate it on pressing the send button.

- Quickly proofread your e-mail to catch any missing words or grammatical and punctuation errors.

- Ensure that your e-mail font size is between 10 pt and 12 pt for easiest readability (either on screen or when printed).

A great habit to get into is to enter the receiver's address last, after the e-mail is complete and ready to be sent. If you're replying, you can simply cut and paste the address into the body of your message for repasting to the address line when the message is ready. In this way, you will never accidentally launch an incomplete or possibly embarrassing message.

Responding to an E-mail

Approximately 65 percent of e-mails require a response. Considerations for responding to a message are quite similar to initiating a new e-mail except for one thing—do you need to respond at all? As we saw in our e-mail ping-pong section, a variety of acknowledgment messages are sent out that serve little if no purpose other than to clog inboxes with trivial items. Therefore, you should be asking yourself two key questions after reviewing an incoming message. Does this message require a response? And if so, does it require an e-mail response?

It's easy for us to pick out the e-mails that you know require responses. Generally, these are requests for information, including decisions and comments. Begin to practice vigilance in outbox management with the remaining electronic messages. E-mails that are truly one-way transmissions of information don't require a response at all—not even a thank you for sending this to me. At one time in e-mail's early days, this was a nice habit and made the application more human. As volumes increased, our tolerances for thank you messages decreased and now they are generally not welcome.

Another practice that should be eliminated from your outbox repertoire is acknowledging receipt of e-mails. Many people send e-mails to indicate that they received your message and will respond to it in the next few days. This extra step of acknowledging is a time waster for both the sender and the receiver. By now we know that people have different priorities for managing their e-mails—there is no hard and fast rule that says that an e-mail transmission, by virtue of its speed in distribution, should be handled immediately. Don't send someone two e-mails for the same message.

Let's now turn to the second question as to whether an incoming e-mail requires an equivalent response. This consideration is a little trickier. With e-mail, we have become quite used to simply matching the channel and sending back e-mail responses to many messages. Now that you have read this book, you are aware that the critical questions here are whether e-mail was the right channel for this message? And if so, should my response be by e-mail or through another channel such as the telephone or a meeting?

The key here is to let the e-mail content and your own intuition be your guide. As we have seen from Chapter 2 on the legal face of e-mail, a great deal of information is committed to electronic mail that should never be in the first place. If you spot such an e-mail, take the initiative to continue this exchange of information on a higher and a safer level. Instinctively, we know when a conversation is required and simply need to exercise this thinking more often.

Once you have gotten into the habit of scrutinizing your e-mails for their response value, you will be in much better control of your outbox. You will send fewer e-mails and have more time to focus on your day-to-day tasks.

Bear in mind also what you should not do: Never send e-mail when you are irritable or tired. Why? So you don't live to regret it. We all have horror stories about the e-mail that got away from us—the one that we sent when we were ticked off or after we received one from someone else who was ticked off. There is always at least one situation that we vividly remember not because we were so highly charged at the time, but because the receiver of our missive also reacted. The usual reaction, if you work in reasonably close physical proximity (within a two-mile radius), is that this recipient suddenly shows up at your office. That is a sure sign that your message got through loud and clear. Invariably you sit down with the injured receiver and allow her or him to blow off steam a bit at your expense, and then you apologize and blame the e-mail system for being so efficient.

You both get back to your respective tasks at your respective offices, and the sorry episode ends. Right? Not necessarily so. The feelings can linger for days, weeks, even months. That is why we seem so easily to recall the "bad e-mail" situation. It is as if we came under a personal and very pointed attack. Suddenly hot, angry words are flashing up on our monitors and our adrenaline starts to pump in sympathetic rhythm.

The face-to-face meeting to resolve the mess is often the best-case scenario. These awkward circumstances—I'm tired; I'm in a hurry; I'm angry; I don't like your tone; I've got a crisis at home—can lead to the e-mail that may haunt you for a long time.

If you as a sender are creating e-mail while tired or emotional, save the e-mail as a draft message—DON'T SEND IT. Go home, relax, and then sleep on it. The next morning, read the draft and decide if this is the message that you want to send. Most of the time, you will discard the message in its entirety, rewrite it, or set up a meeting instead.

The 12-hour break from work and reviewing your message the next morning can save days of regret and damage control. Never miss an opportunity to delay sending an e-mail that you even suspect the receiving end could misinterpret.

Personal Suggestions

Don't toggle between your professional and personal e-mail accounts to send work-based information. Hotmail and Yahoo accounts are known not only to be virus hotbeds, but also their use can diminish your status in the workplace. If you need to receive information away from the office, speak to your IT department about dialing-in to your work e-mail from home.

Remember that workplace e-mails are considered professional documents, where the information should be center-stage. Refrain from using flowery templates, insipid auto-signatures, and sharing your personal philosophy-du-jour; save these for your home e-mail.

Finally, before you press send . . .

Set aside small chunks of time throughout the day to focus on the task of responding to your e-mails. It is much better to apply 10 minutes of focused concentration rather than letting e-mail responses be your never-ending specter throughout the day.

Don't try to multitask by answering e-mails while on the telephone or during small group meetings. There are people who use their Blackberries during larger meetings as an outbox management strategy. It works, but some people think this is rude and callous behavior; it's probably far better to have shorter meetings and spend some of the extra time to focus on separate communication tasks. If this is not possible, then do what one executive has suggested to me and schedule "Blackberry moments," for a five-minute period every hour.

When responding to an e-mail sent to a group, always remember to send your message to the original sender, *not* the group.

Feel free to turn off the sound or text feature that signifies that you have a new e-mail. While some of you may require this degree of urgency, most of us do not. We know there are e-mails waiting for us, so why do we need further intrusive reminders that pressure us to react and respond?

Sender Offenses—A Reminder

So far we have walked through the mechanics of sending clear, concise e-mails—important tools for electronic messaging. This is a critical part of communicating effectively. Another critical part in this equation is our motivation and attitude toward communicating. What are the circumstances that inspire us to engage in the act of sending? As we well know, not all motivations are equal, and that includes ours for e-mail.

We are so intimately involved with e-mail communication that use of the device has become a quirky extension of our personalities. Patterns start to form in our minds about certain senders. Nowadays, no assessment of a coworker is complete without considering their electronic mail habits. Sending certain types of e-mails offends people. These e-mails may be clear, concise, and grammatically correct, yet it is the intended or expressed behavior that puts people off.

While I was writing this book, just this type of incident occurred. Here is an example of what I mean: An employee took it upon himself to meet with the company president to express his disagreement with proposed plans for next year. Afterward, he documented details of this private meeting and sent it to all employees in his department—soon it was spread throughout the company. And soon thereafter, managers were deluged with employee comments expressing their upset and anger over this e-mail—they were embarrassed by the content. This e-mail could easily be interpreted as a reflection of their collective views, when indeed it was not. People also felt somewhat betrayed—their names were put on a controversial e-mail without their prior knowledge or permission.

One option considered was the termination of the employee for unprofessional conduct. But as you can see, regardless of the final outcome, the damage was done and his e-mail sender actions will not be quickly forgotten.

The key things to remember to help reduce sender offenses are:

1. *For each e-mail that you want to send, ask yourself why the other person(s) should receive it.* It sounds simple, but so is pressing the send button. Sometimes we think, "Oh well, if they don't want the information, they can just delete it." Most people get a dozen of these types of e-mails every day—should you contribute to their delete folder?

2. *Use e-mail features judiciously.* Large audience functions like copying, reply to all, and distribution lists are so efficient for sending the same message to multiple parties—they are also the most abused. If you must "copy-in" people to your e-mail, make sure that they

clearly understand why you have chosen to do so. This takes more time than simply pressing send, but so should anything worth communicating well.

3. *Don't let communication by e-mail lull you into a false sense of security.* E-mail is not a sanctuary for your private thoughts. It needs to be used with the same type of considered caution that we would exercise in face-to-face, team, or client meetings. Not everyone gets to say everything that is on his or her mind—don't let e-mail carry you over this edge.

As we saw with the example, there are ways to deal with sender offenses. As in use of our inbox junk filters, where we take control after the fact by ensuring nothing more appears emanating from that particular address, offender victims can also do their parts as good e-mail citizens after an unwanted e-mail is received. Here is another example.

A sender posts an all-campus e-mail . . .

Housmeate Wanted!!
One roommate needed to share
Beautiful home with
Four second-year students

For more information contact Jonathan
At a campus extension or by e-mail

Several hundred people who work on this campus, not those attending classes, which would have been the most logical audience, received the message. Notice that the very first word is misspelled. What happened here was that one recipient took it upon himself to take action in two ways. First, he contacted the IT administrators on campus and asked them to deal directly with this user. Then, he went one step further and sent the following message to the offending sender.

"I have notified the IT administrators and have asked them to deal with this abuse of the system. Jonathan, you have no business using your campus account to send out this kind of stuff, and you have no business sending e-mail to so many users trying to sucker someone into living with you."

It's not a perfect solution. But as we can see, there are ways that we can take control and manage these situations. The benefit is not only in the pushing back, but also in reminding us of the types of sending behaviors that we should avoid in our workplaces. If you practice sending only what needs to be sent, not what you think you want others to receive, we might just learn to love e-mail a little more.

What we have covered so far in this chapter is a common sense approach for initiating and responding to e-mails, and we have offered a proper sense of context for outgoing e-mail. But it is equally important to evaluate the content of the e-mails you send, so in the next section we'll explore the principles of effective communication.

Throughout this book there has been an underlying theme of crafting messages that make life easier for the receiver to not only read and comprehend, but also to respond. Even though there is no obvious rating scale for a well-thought-out message, over time, these do create a lasting impression—one of competence and overall capability. An example of this is the division president who constantly received e-mails from one of her senior vice presidents that were brief phrases with no sentence structure. As time went on, this president began to question this employee's competence in other areas as well. As with any other exchange with coworkers, our e-mails leave an indelible mark.

Communication is a highly prized skill in the workplace, and one we at times seem to take for granted. A 1999 study of *Fortune* 500 companies by Hay Management International revealed that one of the most valued leadership skills found among top performing companies was, you guessed it, the ability to communicate in all directions within the workplace.

E-mail is not just another form of communication, but because of its frequent use in the workplace, it is an important channel to master. With this in mind, the next section provides a refresher on how to create effective, powerful, and career-enhancing e-mails.

COMMUNICATING EFFECTIVELY

Have you ever been involved in an exercise where a message is passed verbally from one person to another? The exercise works as follows: put 6 to 7 people in a room, create a brief message and whisper it into the first person's ear, ensuring no one else hears it. That person then whispers the exact message to the next person and so on. For those of you who have been through this type of exercise, you know that by the time the message gets to the last person, who then repeats what they just heard out loud, there is no similarity at all to the original message. This is a comical, but classic example of how easily meanings can be interpreted and thereby altered in our minds as they are communicated onwards.

Now taking this into the workplace, imagine that you are a manager, and a meeting takes place with a dozen people in the room. Discussions ensue and the meeting adjourns. Hours later, a casual discussion with others who attended the same meeting, reveal there are significant differences in what they understand as the meeting's intent and its outcome. Everyone seemed to be paying attention, taking notes, and asking questions—everything seemed to be in order; except for one thing—a shared understanding of the situation. What happened here is that people in the meeting were hearing but not listening. We mistakenly tend to assume that the two acts are synonymous—they are not. Hearing is the fundamental human function we tap into to facilitate listening, which we can define as a higher order mechanism that creates understanding. If there is no clear purpose being conveyed in the meeting and no clearly delineated outcomes, then it doesn't matter how many notes people take or how long the meeting lasts, there will be no collective or shared understanding after the meeting adjourns.

We all know how easily misunderstandings in communication can and do occur. Many times we simply take this for granted and assume that if we are speaking then indeed the audience must understand our words. For example, a lecturer walks into a classroom and begins his presentation. Five minutes later, he asks a question of the group and there is no response. At that moment, another lecturer rushes into the classroom and says to his perplexed colleague, "Thanks for starting the class—I didn't know you could speak Dutch." What we see from this example is that in the first five minutes, there was only communication between two audiences without any connection. The moment the lecturer learned that the class did not understand his language, was the moment there was a shared understanding of the situation.

Almost as important as speaking the same language is the ability to connect with your audience. These stories show us how easily misunderstandings in communication can and do occur. We rest on the notion that if we can read, write, and speak, we can communicate, but as we can see from these examples, this is often not enough to create a shared understanding. As the parent of any teenager will attest, trying to communicate despite different styles and agendas is very difficult but well worth the effort. It is the same with e-mail at work; we need to overcome the compositional challenge to get the real work done.

Over 2,000 years ago, rhetoric's founding father Aristotle identified five key public presentation principles that have stood the test of time and become touchstones for sound communication. These canons were invention (the logic of the speech), arrangement (the speech's construction), style (articulation of the ideas), delivery (the speaker's manner and tone), and memory (the speaker's preparation and his or her content knowledge). They provide solid guidance in our attempts to communicate effectively over e-mail. We can use them as a backdrop to enhance our thinking and our actions to achieve outbox mastery.

KNOW YOUR AGENDA

The basic purpose of any form of communication is to transfer information in such a manner that the audience receives and understands it. If the audience understands the information presented, it is able to make critical decisions based on the information.

For e-mail, this principle is crucial. The ease of using e-mail often masks the ultimate reason for using it. The act of sending an e-mail is equivalent to presenting information to an intended audience. The key elements we need to consider are why it is being sent in the first place, and what information is being conveyed by the message. Will the e-mail provide information that is easy to comprehend and digest or will it be a morass of words on a monitor?

Outbox Action Items

Subject Line

It's important to sell your message using the subject line. Most people will make their decisions on reading, and responding to your e-mail on this basis. In the last chapter, we covered creating descriptive, action-oriented subject lines. Let's take this a step further by changing subject lines to show the progression in an e-mail exchange.

For example, here are four subject lines relating to the same e-mail message:

1. Request for resources for project X
2. Verification requested—resource request for project X
3. Verification provided—project X
4. Project X—resource request approved

Even though there are text messages accompanying each e-mail, we can see from this progression of subject lines how well the flow of information is being managed on a message-by-message basis. Always make sure that your subject line reflects the nature of your message.

The First Sentence

What you write in the opening of your message must convey what you want the reader to do with this information. This may seem too sudden, but remember that you have an action-oriented subject line that has already prepared the reader for your message.

By all means greet the reader.

Hi Richard, I hope you're doing well.

Hello Marie, it was great to see you last night.

Jordan, it's been a while since we have spoken.

Mr. Haskayne, we have not met.

These are perfectly acceptable and serve to set a pleasant tone to your e-mail. Once you get the pleasantries established, it's time to sum up the objective of your request. This request should be framed in terms of the action you want the reader to undertake on your behalf—this is a hallmark in our principles of effective communication covered earlier in the chapter. Now view the next step in our e-mail construction.

Hi Richard, I hope you're doing well. Could we meet next week to discuss your new project?

Hello Marie, it was great to see you last night. You asked me to remind you to send that article you are working on.

Jordan, it's been a while since we have spoken. Would you have the time to serve on our special task force?

Mr. Haskayne, we have not met, however, I would be grateful for your advice.

In all these situations, whether you know them personally or not, the first sentence has reached out to the reader. Notice that our requested actions are natural and conversational, not wooden such as:

I am writing this e-mail to you to request your action in assisting me with my project.

With e-mail, it's important to keep the tone professional and the words moving in the direction of your request.

KNOW YOUR AUDIENCE

What does your audience need to know and how do you get it interested in what you have to say? The presentation should capture the audience's attention, establish the speaker's credibility, and frame the information in a way that the audience would understand.

An e-mail can capture an audience if it is the right message intended for the right person. The send button should not be seen as a gateway to bring your message to a wider audience. E-mails need to be tailored to their specific receivers. The information in an e-mail captures receiver attention when it is relevant to their work and delivered in a timely fashion. Greater care in this area would significantly reduce workplace e-mail traffic. The ability to send messages to multiple parties is seen as a great benefit of the e-mail system. Using wide-audience features such as cc, reply to-all, and distribution lists, are not.

Outbox Action Items

Engage your audience by showing that you are considering their point of view and not only your own. We'll use the examples from the previous section:

> Hi Richard, I hope you're doing well. I want to meet next week to discuss your new project.
>
> Hello Marie, it was great to see you last night. Send me that article.
>
> Jordan, it's been a while since we have spoken. I have put your name forward to serve on our special task force.
>
> Mr. Haskayne, we have not met. I want your advice.

The messages seem the same as was used in the first sentence section, but are they? Compare them. The collegial tone is gone, and has been replaced with an undertone that says my needs come first. It seems subtle, but which message would you rather receive?

I want to meet with you (!) or Could we meet (?)

I inserted the exclamation point and the question mark to further emphasize the implied tone of these two similar requests. As we can see, a powerful tool in your sending arsenal is to use language that is focused on your reader's time and inclinations, not on yours.

STRUCTURE THE MESSAGE

Create a body of information that is logical and compelling. How ideas are presented is as important as the ideas themselves. Many highly technical presentations fail to fulfill this principle simply because one idea jumps to the next; in the same way, e-mails should be written as if approaching the material for the first time.

Generally, e-mails are short messages conveying specific information. Receivers expect to spend seconds, not minutes in judging the content of a message. Therefore, e-mails need to come to the point right away. As we saw with the subject line and first sentence, the entire message should be designed to convey high-impact information. E-mails that hold us hostage by reversing this order create tension and waste time.

Outbox Action Items

Take care in laying out the information in your e-mails. Use paragraphs, subheadings, bolded key words, and bullet points to add emphasis and make the message more readable. These same principles apply to e-mail messages.

Which one of these vendor messages is easier to read?

Your Web sites and online publications add strategic value when the content, attitude, writing style, and design dimensions comprehensively create the desired level of virtual integration you need to build a sustainable competitive advantage for your business.

We provide online interactive storefronts and documentation featuring online technical documentations, newsletters, brochures, demos, and other special interest online multimedia business communications products you can share with your customers, suppliers, and employees to increase the strategic value of your business.

or . . .

Give your business a competitive advantage by allowing us to create your Web sites and online publications. We provide the following services:

- Online interactive storefronts
- Technical documentation
- Newsletters
- Brochures

Our company designs business communication products you can share with customers, suppliers, and employees to increase the value of your business.

Most people prefer the second version because the objective (a sales pitch) is in the first sentence, and the key elements of the message are highlighted with bullet points. Notice too that a more direct form of writing, without flowery business jargon, is inherently shorter and easier for the reader to comprehend.

Another tip for keeping your messages structured is to use shorter sentences. The shorter the sentence, the easier it is for us to understand its meaning. In a study by the American Press Institute, a sentence with 19 words has an 80 percent comprehension rate, whereas a sentence with 8 words has 100 percent comprehension—true support for the case where less is really more.

KEEP IT SIMPLE

E-mail messages should provide a seamless blend of images and text. To achieve this, it's important to create visuals that are highly informative, not highly designed.

Using e-mail should be a choice for conveying information, not a default. Is e-mail the right medium for the message or should it be delivered using another medium. There is no doubt that we can put any and every message into text form. This does not mean that we should. The availability and easy access of e-mail should not be confused with providing the correct platform for a message. We may frustrate our ability to structure an effective message especially for more complex ideas. This is particularly true in information that requires a fuller expression between parties such as concepts and ideas. This is also true with sending attachments, as proxies for presentations, which are too dense to be stand-alone information.

Outbox Action Items

We know that e-mail permits us to share, almost effortlessly, any and all types of electronic-based information. We also know that this functionality is overused and does nothing but clog up others' inboxes. As a personal audit, ask yourself whether you need to send:

- The *entire* e-mail thread
- That attachment or web link
- The message acknowledging receipt
- The items forwarded to you

A quick check on these items, especially from the perspective of the receiving party, will do wonders for your e-mail sending profile. This is another situation where less is really more. As with creating new subject lines for each e-mail, try and keep your underlying messages refreshed and spanking clean of superfluous materials.

In addition, in our richly graphic and visual world, it's become all to easy to use images and short forms to convey meaning. Acronyms, symbols, and emoticons (a short form of the two words *emotion icon*), have been all the rage within certain circles, usually outside the workplace. Indeed, even the acronym TLA, which means "three-letter acronym" is abbreviated.

For those of us who are acquainted with these items, my advice is to not use them in the workplace. Not only are they considered by many to be unprofessional, but the vast majority of workplace e-mail users don't even know what some of these are:

Typical symbols	Smiley faces. ☺ ☹
Emoticons	Typing keystrokes combined to set mood, such as :-) (happy) or :-((sad).
Acronyms	Generally three letter groups that are short forms for common phrases: BTW—by the way, JMO—just my opinion, OTT—over the top.

It's far better to create good tone and understanding in your e-mails by spelling out your message. Use of symbols will only serve to confuse the message, possibly taking it out of context.

KNOW YOUR SUBJECT

Aristotle held that speakers should be well prepared and re-hearsed so that they can easily depart from the planned flow of the presentation if needed. At a moment's notice, they should be able to discuss related issues that the audience raises or reframe the original dialog in different ways.

In our cut-and-paste world, it is far too easy to put materials into an e-mail that are not original nor an expression of your own views. Just as in presentations that are too rehearsed, the audience may begin to suspect that e-mail information is out of character for the sender's knowledge level. In these situations, the receiver is more apt to follow up on the information to sat-isfy themselves that it is genuine. The inability of a sender to support his or her e-mail or provide greater context during a conversation, will cast doubt not only on the current situation, but also on subsequent ones.

Outbox Action Items

Generally, e-mails should be matter-of-fact exchanges of information—they should be *personable*, not personal. I often think of John F. Kennedy's words "civility is not a weakness, and sincerity is subject to proof," when trying to convey to people the importance of tone in their e-mail messages. The words we choose to use in any given situation can sting—multiply this tenfold when these words appear nakedly on our monitors.

The big problem here is that only our words can be used to convey the message—there are no nonverbal clues to assist us in promoting our exact meaning. Phrases like "you don't understand, you state that, you forgot to, or you claim that," come across quite differently when spoken versus written. It's the same with sentences that contain "how dare you, if you had called, you can't do that, and from now on." Use of these phrases can begin to smack of computer-rage. Even if you as the sender do not intend this to happen, there is no doubt that in seeing these types of phrases, the receiver will reinterpret your meaning.

Although this has been mentioned in Chapter 1, this also relates to our ability to keep the message simple. Those times that your hands are hovering over the keyboard unable to type, should be a signal to you that you are either too mentally tired to develop an e-mail or that your message needs to be verbally delivered.

Refrain from using language in your e-mails that may be the least bit contentious. It takes focus to craft a good e-mail. Be cognizant of the ramifications of sending careless e-mails. It's far better not to send a message when you have any doubts as to its shared meaning, so never force yourself to compose and send.

ON THE TIMELESSNESS OF COMMUNICATING WELL

In comparing e-mail, our newest communication channel, to the time-worn principles of public presentation, we can see a pattern emerge: E-mail may be quick and cheap, but its use implies creating that all-important shared understanding. This understanding begins with a clear purpose for a message that is matched against the receivers' needs. We further promote our adherence to this understanding through selecting the right channel. We then cement our communication contract through taking the care to structure the information for easy reading and action. The overall impression, then, is a credible message that's easily understood.

Presentations that do not strike the right chord with audiences are immediately noticed. The level of response or reaction is usually low. We can now see that sending a poorly composed e-mail can have the same impact. What makes this an even greater issue than in presentations is exposure—we send many more e-mails throughout a work week. This gives us a regular opportunity to show our clients and coworkers whether we are able to create shared understanding through our electronic messages.

Ask yourself how you feel when an e-mail message from a colleague or superior is quickly followed-up with a second message correcting and clarifying the initial information. When this happens a second or third time, even in the span of six months, we recall that this has happened before and therefore give less credence to these messages. We begin to implicitly feel that our time is not being respected or valued. We may also reflect on those individuals' capabilities in other areas. What this shows us is that the e-mail application is easy to use, yet must be handled with the same caution we would exercise in dealing with important client communication.

This brings us to the end of communicating effectively, which you can also call your personal e-mail workshop. Hopefully you glided effortlessly through these key steps, fully appreciating the value of the nuances in outbox supremacy. As you can see, the devil is truly in the details. You now know the subtleties required in crafting solid, well-intentioned messages. Keep this guide marked and handy, so you can refer readily to it in future.

INSTANT MESSAGING

Instant messaging (IM) is making its way into workplaces in an unofficial capacity. It is the closest thing we have to fully synchronous electronic communication. The beauty of IM is that most compositional formalities covered in this chapter are, by nature of the technology alone, definitely not applicable. IM is strictly an informal communication subchannel— almost the antithesis of e-mail.

Currently, IM has three problems in the workplace. First, it's still considered an underground form of communication, which for the most part, is not supported nor condoned in many organizations. There is a perception that IM's use in the workplace will hamper employee productivity because people will use it strictly for social purposes.

Second, IM in its current configuration is both a security risk and a spam magnet. When we open an IM window, it creates a port or a hole through corporate firewalls that exposes the entire network to risk of attack by a variety of professional hackers. IM systems can transfer infected files at lightning speed and this feature makes it very attractive to virus writers. IM spam interrupts users in the middle of conversations, creating high levels of dissatisfaction and frustration among IM's most ardent users.

Third, organizational response is mixed at best. Some companies have studied current IM systems and have deemed them too risky or inadequate to protect their multibillion dollar investments in system security. Other companies actively block access to IM. The remaining companies, which I estimate to be more than 50 percent, may not even be aware of the extent to which IM is used in their workplaces. In these cases, it seems that IT departments find out the hard way through sudden, stronger than usual virus attacks.

At this point, IM is a nascent technology, but one whose use is sure to grow in the workplace. The advantages that robust IM systems will provide in the future are (1) built-in storage and archiving of communications that will make legal retrievals faster and much cheaper, (2) real time efficiency and speed among similarly connected public and business networks, and (3) fewer e-mails.

In the meantime, here are some interim tips to help with IM use and acceptability in the workplace.

Tips for Individual IM Users

1. Remember that IM use, especially through free public applications, is not secure. Don't post anything that could be considered sensitive or protected company information.

2. Restrict your buddy list at work to coworkers, not social contacts. This helps to promote IM use at the workplace for these activities.

3. Respect and accept company policies on blocking IM. There are valid security risks that need to be resolved

with this capability. Use IM blocking as a reason to interact more through the telephone or in person.

Tips for Organizations

1. Investigate IM use within your company to learn if it is being used, for what purpose, and by which work groups.
2. Evaluate the impact of IM on workgroup collaborations and on potential distractions.
3. Use this information to develop a strategy for how your organization would most appropriately use IM.
4. Keep apprized of enterprise-wide IM technologies in current development.

This chapter captured the key elements you need to consider when sending an e-mail or an instant message. The information in this chapter gives you the tools to plan, create, and execute superior, high-content e-mails. It can also be used and applied to all other types of communication that you use at work and in your personal life. As we have seen throughout this book, good communication doesn't occur naturally—it is learned. You now have the means to improve and hone your skills in this area.

The information in this book is designed to serve your needs in two ways: to enlighten you on the problems that you face every day and provide a continued reference point in searching for the answers. The answers to reducing e-mail volumes and our resulting workplace stresses are not the sole domain of the individual worker or the organization—both must play an integral role to truly achieve long-term success.

CHAPTER 6

The Smoking Gun

This final chapter summarizes the key points presented in this book, reinforces the benefits of taking action, and provides a road map so you can get started.

Chapter 1 showed us how we work differently when we use e-mail, and as with many problems in life, naming them is the first step in solving them. That is, by understanding the expectations and common behaviors that e-mail brings out in us, we should have a better idea of how to use it more effectively overall. Reducing e-mail traffic is one of the biggest hurdles, and one that will have a direct and immediate impact on corporate profitability.

In Chapter 2, we discovered how vulnerable our e-mails are. Knowing this helps us decide what types of information we should commit to e-mail, and what is best left in other forms.

The key lesson from Chapter 3 is that matching the medium to the message is critical. We've explored how choosing the wrong communication channel can be counterproductive, and learned how to choose an appropriate medium for each piece of information.

Chapter 4 was a guided tour through the common pitfalls of dealing with a high volume of messages. It provided practical advice about how to distinguish the high-content messages you want while helping to solve the problem of too much low-value information. It uncovered the timesaving features of most e-mail applications and explored the diagnostic steps that department managers and organizations can take to assess the extent of e-mail problems in their workplaces.

Chapter 5 acted as a mirror to Chapter 4. While most of us know how frustrating it is to read a poorly conceived message, it's not so easy to be a model citizen in this regard. In this chapter, we showed how a firm grounding in the basics of good communication techniques helps you create information-rich, concise e-mails.

I hope that you put the tools in these chapters to work.

E-mail's popularity in the workplace has moved the art of written communication back to center stage. However, this writing resurgence has uncovered some fundamental problems with communication at work. While poorly written memos are becoming less tolerable, supervisors of the offending parties often have little time to spend to show us the way. Rather than simply accepting mediocrity in workplace communications, organizations should create and hold employees to a higher standard for all written documentation, and now especially for e-mail.

An important caveat to consider is that no matter how advanced our communication technologies become—be they electronic paper, voice-initiated typing, or anything else that our imaginations can concoct—these inventions will not change the substance of *what* we communicate; they will change only *how* we communicate. The rationale for introducing Aristotle's ideals for effective communication is that in 2,500 years, not much has changed. Our expectations for receiver-centered communication still remain the same.

Technological advances in communication have shown us how easily we can be led astray by its inappropriate use, while at the same time highlighting our own inherent deficiencies. Perhaps this is one of e-mail's greatest legacies—it gives us the means to initiate a process for stronger and better communication in our workplaces, where both individuals and organizations benefit. It gives us a "smoking gun."

People have become concerned enough to actively seek remedies. Yet, the purported solutions on offer—sorters, multiple in-boxes, word-recognition software, and other anti-spam devices—are based solely on technological functionality and don't change unproductive user habits. Because of the larger e-mail issue of effective use as a communication channel, it is totally up to individuals, managers, and organizations to move beyond the sophomoric use of e-mail and start thinking outside the inbox.

With this ideal firmly rooted in our minds, here is one last guide that sets your thinking on the right path to e-mail success.

Individuals

On your own, you can take control over what appears in your inbox and become a model e-mail user—both by what you send and what you choose not to send. You can initiate your own personal guidelines on appropriate e-mail use. You can share these with the people responsible for formal training to help impact the entire organization. Talk to your coworkers when you get an e-mail that could be improved in tone or content. More highly motivated individuals can develop and execute training for electronic mail senders on the context and content for effective e-mailing, in addition to providing additional information on use of the application itself.

Management

Begin by embracing the tenets in this book and be a role model for using all communication channels in their proper place and time. Fortify these actions by being an advocate for the development and reinforcement of e-mail guidelines. You can then create awareness, through discussion and initiating training on reducing dependence on electronic communication and increasing use of other channels. Actively seek out better practices in other departments or companies and be on the lookout for e-mail transgressions or worst practices. Support your employees' individual actions for creating a better e-mailing environment.

Organizational Leaders

Recognize that e-mail is a valuable corporate resource that can be managed productively to achieve (1) better bottom-line results, (2) greater security of information, and (3) improved employee satisfaction. Understand that overuse of the e-mail system costs millions of dollars every year in time spent on low-value messages that divert employee time and attention from profit-generating activities. Make the e-mail system perform for you and show you its real worth; create benchmarks, test them, measure them, question them, improve them. Well-informed corporate cultures drive superior performance and superior results. Therefore, seek to proactively support reduction of unnecessary e-mail volumes by at least 25 percent per year, 50 percent if it can be managed over the next couple of years. These actions will add excellent value to your company resulting in better margins and improved return on your resources.

PARTING WORDS

There is no doubt that e-mail is central to our work lives. It keeps us connected to our organizations and connected to new business opportunities. Your next e-mail, well structured, could be the starting point for a million-dollar business deal. Your next e-mail, poorly structured, could mean that your name is dropped from a high-profile project. E-mail is ubiquitous, but that does not make it risk-free. Every time that we send one, we are making an impression.

As an originator of corporation-wide e-mail to all employees, do you want the company to see your department as ineffective because your e-mails are too verbose, or missing critical information? As a manager, do you want to be seen as an effective employee or an e-mail addict? As an executive, do you want the harsh but silent judgment of subordinates who think your e-mails rambling, unstructured streams of consciousness? No one wants to see these things happen, but they take place in many North American offices every day. That is part of the massive power of e-mail. The power to send is transcended only by the power to make a negative impression. The power to avoid these mishaps is now in your hands, and I invite you to visit my web site, www.christinacavanagh.com, for updates and future insights into e-mail.

This book highlighted the most common problems and frustrations we encounter when we use e-mail; it was designed to help you integrate your electronic arsenal more efficiently into your job functions. By thinking outside the inbox, we can make workplace e-mailing a much more pleasant and productive experience. It is my sincere hope that this book has assisted you in finding a level of skill and comfort with e-mail that makes you that much more effective at what you do!

REFERENCES

Baldassano, Valli, and Roy Speed. "Bad Documents Can Kill You." *Across the Board* 38 (2001): 46–51.

Cavanagh, Christina A. *E-mail in the Workplace: Testing for E-mail Relevance*, March 2000.

Cavanagh, Christina A. *E-mail in the Workplace: Discovering Unproductive Practices*, September 2001.

Cavanagh, Christina A. *E-mail in the Workplace: A Productivity Study*, June 2002.

Conlin, Michelle. "Watch What You Put in the Office E-mail." *Business Week* (30 September 2002): 114.

Craig, Susanne, and Ann Davis. "UBS Warburg Is Ordered to Pay for Retrieval of E-mails in Case." *Wall Street Journal Online* (19 May 2003).

Daft, Richard L., and Robert H. Lengel. "Information Richness: A New Approach to Managerial Behaviour and Organizational Design." *Research in Organizational Behaviour* 6 (1984): 191–233.

Department of Justice, Government of Canada. "Lawful Access—Consultation Document." August 2002. http:// www.canada.justice.gc.ca/en/cons/la_al.

Department of Justice, United States of America. Appendix to *Searching and Seizing Computers and Obtaining Electronic Evidence in Criminal Investigations.* http://www.usdoj.gov /criminal/cybercrime/s&sappendix2002.htm (accessed 9 December 2002).

DiGilio, John J. "Electronic Mail: From Computer to Courtroom." *Information Management Journal* 35 (2001): 32–44.

Gladwell, Malcolm. "The Social Life of Paper: Looking for Method in the Mess." http://www.gladwell.com/2002 /2002_03_25_a_paper.htm.

Glasner, Joanna. "IM Bans Hush Workplace Chatter." *Wired News.* September 17, 2002. http://www.wired.com/news /business/0,1367,55090,00.html (sourced 14 March 2003).

Goddard, Robert W. "Communication: Use Language Effectively." *Personnel Journal* (April 1989): 32–36.

Greenwald, Judy. "E-mails Constitute Trespassing." *Court Business Insurance* 35 (2001): 2, 31.

Griffin, Emory A. *A First Look at Communication Theory. 3rd ed.* New York: McGraw-Hill, 1997.

Hafner, Katie. "Billions Served Daily and Counting." *New York Times* (6 December 2001): Circuits.

Hallowell, Edward M. "The Human Moment at Work." *Harvard Business Review* (January/February 1999): 58–66.

Harmon, Amy. "Clique of Instant Messagers Expands Into the Workplace." *New York Times* (11 March 2003).

Hayes, Mary. "E-discovery Eases the Paper Chase." *Information Week* 903 (2002): 58–61.

Haythornthwaite, Caroline, and Barry Wellman. "Work, Friendship, and Media Use for Information Exchange in a Networked Organization." *Journal of the American Society for Information Science* 49 (1998): 1101–1114.

Headlam, Bruce. "How to E-mail Like a CEO." *New York Times* (8 April 2001).

Hertz, Frederick. "Don't Let Your Case Get Lost in an E-mail." *New Jersey Law Journal* 169 (2 September 2002).

Hilton, Denis J. "The Social Context of Reasoning: Conversational Inference and Rational Judgment." *Psychological Bulletin* 118 (1995): 248–271.

Isaacs, Ellen, Alan Walendowski, Steve Whittaker, Diane J. Schiano, and Candace Kamm. "The Character, Functions, and Styles of Instant Messaging in the Workplace." *Proceedings of CSCW '02*, November 16–20, 2002, New Orleans, Louisiana, U.S.A.

Jackson, Tom, R. Dawson, and D. Wilson. "Improving the Communications Process: The Costs and Effectiveness of E-mail Compared with Traditional Media." Paper presented at the Inspire 2000 Conference, U.K., June 1999.

Jackson, Tom, R. Dawson, and D. Wilson. "The Cost of E-mail Interruption." Research paper, Loughborough University, Leicestershire, U.K., 2000.

Kemper, Cynthia L. "Backlash." *Communication World* 17 (2000): 22–25.

Kornblum, Janet. "Spam? No Thanks, We're Full." *NewsFactor Network*. http://www.newsfactor.com/perl/story/20447.html (sourced 21 January 2003).

Lash, Rick. "Top Leadership: Taking the Inner Journey." *Ivey Business Journal* (May/June 2002): 44–48.

Loomis, Tamara. "Company E-mail: Electronic Messages Can Become Damaging Evidence." *New York Law Journal* 225 (8 February 2001).

Markus, M. L. "Electronic Mail as the Medium of Managerial Choice." *Organization Science.* 5 (1994): 502–527.

Mason, Kate. "You've Got (Too Much) Mail." *Target Marketing* 24 (2001): 22.

Matthews, Virginia. "E-mail Truths Reveal Much about Management Style." *FT.com* (13 February 2002).

McLuhan, Marshall, and Edmund S. Carpenter. *Explorations in Communication.* Boston: Beacon Press, 1960.

McLuhan, Marshall. *Understanding Media: The Extensions of Man.* New York: McGraw-Hill, 1964.

McLuhan, Marshall. *The Medium Is the Massage: An Inventory of Effects.* New York: Bantam, 1967.

Mintzberg, Henry. *The Nature of Managerial Work.* New York: Harper & Row, 1973.

Moulton, Donalee. "Workplace E-mail Raises Liability, Privacy Concerns." *Lawyer's Weekly* 20 (23 February 2001).

Neuliep, James William. *Human Communication Theory: Applications and Case Studies.* Massachusetts: Allyn & Bacon, 1996.

Odiorne, George S. "MBO Means Having a Goal and a Plan Not Just a Goal." *Manage* 44 (1992): 8–10.

Paddock, Robert L. "Utilizing E-mail as Business Records under the Texas Rules of Evidence." *HeinOnline* 19 Rev. Litig. 61 (2000).

Poirier, Marc-Alexandre. "Employer Monitoring of the Corporate E-mail System: How Much Privacy Can Employees Reasonably Expect." *University of Toronto Faculty of Law Review* 60 (2002): 85–104.

Romm, Celia T., and Nava Pliskin. "The Office Tyrant— Social Control through E-mail." *Information Technology and People* 12 (1999): 27–43.

Schwartz, David G. "Shared Semantics and the Use of Organizational Memories for E-mail Communications." *Internet Research: Electronic Networking Applications and Policy* 8 (1998): 434–441.

Schwarz, Norbert. "Judgement in a Social Context: Biases, Shortcomings, and the Logic of Conversation." *Advances in Experimental Social Psychology* 26 (1994): 123–162.

Scully, Daniel J., and Mary Dirkes. "Can E-mail Be Protected by Attorney-Client Privilege?" *Defense Counsel Journal* 66 (1999): 281–285.

Sellen, Abigail J., and Richard H. R. Harper. *The Myth of the Paperless Office*. Cambridge: Massachusetts Institute of Technology, 2002.

Simmons, Donald B. "The Nature of the Organizational Grapevine." *Supervisory Management* (November 1985): 40.

Speier, Cheri, Joseph S. Valacich, and Iris Vessey. "The Influence of Task Interruption on Individual Decision Making: An Information Overload Perspective." *Decision Sciences* 30 (1999): 337–360.

Trevino, Linda K., Robert H. Lengel, and Richard L. Daft. "Media Symbolism, Media Richness and Media Choice in Organizations: A Symbolic Interactionist Perspective." *Communication Research* 14 (1987): 553–574.

Tolson, Bill. "Controlling the Flood." *Computer Technology Review* 22 (2002): 16.

Tuten, Tracy L., David J. Urban, and George Gray. "Electronic Mail as Social Influence in Downsized Organizations." *Human Resource Management* 37 (1998): 249–261.

Yankelovich, Daniel. *The Magic of Dialogue: Transforming Conflict into Cooperation*. New York: Simon & Schuster, 1999.

INDEX